Delivered
From the Wrath to Come

A Study of the Pretribulational Rapture

J. A. Moorman

Delivered from the Wrath to Come

ISBN 978-1-7321746-1-0

All Scripture quotes are from the King James Bible.

Address All Inquiries To:
THE OLD PATHS PUBLICATIONS, INC.
142 Gold Flume Way
Cleveland, Georgia, U.S.A.
Web: www.theoldpathspublications.com
E-mail: TOP@theoldpathspublications.com

DEDICATION

To Colin Tyler:

A faithful servant of Christ for many years in the Midlands of England. A defender of the King James Bible and preacher of the Imminent Return of Jesus Christ. One of the faithful few. May God continue to bless his ministry in these last days.

J. A. Moorman
August, 2018

TABLE OF CONTENTS

OUTLINE

I. The Nature of the Tribulation
    A. Designations of the Tribulation
        1. A Time of Trouble Like None Other
        2. The Day of the Lord
        3. A Time of God's Wrath and Indignation
    B. Purposes of the Tribulation
        1. To Prepare Israel for Her Messiah
        2. To Punish the World
    C. Timing of the Tribulation
        1. It is Connected with the Return of Christ
        2. Its Duration will be Seven Years
    D. Reality of the Tribulation

II. The Rapture and Return Contrasted From Scripture
    A. The Rapture of the Church
        1. Believers Caught Up, Gathered, In Christ's Presence, Delivered from Wrath
        2. Imminent Expectancy of Christ's Return
        3. Allusions to the Rapture
    B. The Return of Christ to Earth
        1. From Genesis to Psalms
        2. From Isaiah to Daniel
        3. From Hosea to Malachi
        4. From the Gospels and Acts
        5. From Romans to Revelation

III. Reasons For The Pretribulational Rapture
    A. Ten Basic Reasons
    B. Fifty Reasons by John Walvoord
        1. Historical Argument
        2. Interpretational Argument
        3. Nature of the Tribulation
        4. Nature of the Church
        5. Doctrine of Imminency
        6. The Work of the Holy Spirit

    7. Necessity of an Interval Between the Rapture
       and the Second Coming

    8. Contrasts Between the Rapture and the Second
       Coming

**C. Further Reasoning for the Pretribulation
Rapture**

    1. The Rapture Is Not Timed, The Revelation Is Timed

    2. The Rapture is Clearly Intimated in the Gospels

    3. The Rapture and the Last Trumpet

    4. The *Day of Christ* in II Thessalonians 2

    5. The Restated Events in II Thessalonians

    6. A Posttribulational Rapture is Contradictory

INTRODUCTION

Christ is coming again! As S. Franklin Logsdon, greatly used Bible teacher of a past generation, wrote: "This marvellous fact has a magnitude of abounding proportions and a magnetism of captivating force. It is a fact established with convincing and reassuring impressiveness. All prophecy either directly or indirectly, revolves around the return of Christ who will deal with the Church, with Israel, and with the nations. *I will come again*, is **His personal promise** (Jhn 14:3). *This same Jesus, whom ye see go into heaven shall so come in like manner*, is **the dramatic corroboration** (Acts 1:11). *The Lord himself shall descend from heaven*, is **the alerting emphasis** (I Thess 4:16)."

In connection with Christ's Second Coming, the Bible describes in great detail the time of glory when Christ will reign literally upon the earth He created and for which He died. Immediately before this time *when the earth shall be full of the knowledge of the Lord as the waters cover the sea* (Isa 11:9), the Bible in equal measure and graphic detail tells of the earth coming under a time of trouble of unparalleled intensity. It is a fearful, calamitous, unprecedented time. It will be **a time when the nations are angry** (Rev 11:18). It will be **a time when the devil is angry**: *Woe to the inhabiters of the earth and of the sea! for the devil is come down unto you, having great wrath, because he knoweth that he hath but a short time* (Rev 12:12). But the wrath of the nations and Satan are only consequential as God may use these in the execution of His will, for it is **the time of God's anger.** In those days earth will be placed under the wrath of God. It is called the Tribulation, the 70th Week of Daniel, the Day of the Lord. Man's day is now over. The Lord's Day has come. The true believing Church will ***not*** be on earth during that time.

The Promise Given to the Believing Church

Because thou hast kept the word of my patience, I also will keep thee from the hour of temptation, which shall come upon all the world, to try them that dwell upon the earth. Revelation 3:10.

<u>One</u>: An *hour of temptation is coming*. It is an *hour* in comparison to the *ages* of general tribulation that have fallen on parts of the earth. It is an *hour*, only a short time, yet an exceedingly intense time. It contains more tribulation than that of all the previous ages combined.

<u>Two</u>: It will be *upon all the earth*. It will not be in only the "trouble spots" of the earth; the entire earth will feel the full weight of its fury.

<u>Three</u>: Those who *kept the word of his patience* during times of *general* tribulation will be *kept from* the time of *great* tribulation. During these times of general tribulation, faith is exercised to wait in *patience* for His Return: *Be **patient** therefore, brethren, unto the coming of the Lord. Behold, the husbandman waiteth for the precious fruit of the earth, and hath **long patience** for it, until he receive the early and latter rain* (Jms 5:7).

<u>Four</u>: Believers will be *kept from* (Gr. *ek*) the terrible hour. They will not go *through* it, but will be kept *from* it. This is a key passage demonstrating that the Rapture of believers will take place before the terrible time of trouble. The coming Tribulation is one unit composed of Seven Seals containing Seven Trumpets and Seven Vials. We will not go through any part of it.

CHAPTER 1
The Nature of the Tribulation

A. Designations of the Tribulation

1. A Time of Trouble Like None Other

Five times the Bible specifically declares that this will be a time of trouble like none the world has ever experienced. It will be a time beyond comparison. The prophetic Scriptures culminating with the Book of Revelation unite in pointing to this time.

> • *Alas! for that day is great, so that **none is like it**: it is even the time of Jacob's trouble, but he shall be saved out of it* (Jer 30:7).

> • *And at that time shall Michael stand up, the great prince which standeth for the children of thy people: and there shall be a time of trouble, **such as never was** since there was a nation even to that same time: and at that time thy people shall be delivered, every one that shall be found written in the book* (Dan 12:1).

> • *A day of darkness and of gloominess, a day of clouds and of thick darkness, as the morning spread upon the mountains: a great people and a strong; **there hath not been ever the like,** neither shall be any more after it, even to the years of many generations* (Joel 2:2).

> • *For then shall be great tribulation, **such as was not** since the beginning of the world to this time, no, nor ever shall be* (Matt 24:21).

> • *For in those days shall be affliction, **such as was not** from the beginning of the creation which God created unto this time, neither shall be* (Mk 13:19).

11

2. The Day of the Lord

• *For **the day of the LORD** of hosts shall be upon every one that is proud and lofty, and upon every one that is lifted up; and he shall be brought low* (Isa 2:12).

• *Howl ye; for **the day of the LORD** is at hand; it shall come as a destruction from the Almighty. Therefore shall all hands be faint, and every man's heart shall melt: And they shall be afraid: pangs and sorrows shall take hold of them; they shall be in pain as a woman that travaileth: they shall be amazed one at another; their faces shall be as flames. Behold, **the day of the LORD** cometh, cruel both with wrath and fierce anger, to lay the land desolate: and he shall destroy the sinners thereof out of it. For the stars of heaven and the constellations thereof shall not give their light: the sun shall be darkened in his going forth, and the moon shall not cause her light to shine. And I will punish the world for their evil, and the wicked for their iniquity; and I will cause the arrogancy of the proud to cease, and will lay low the haughtiness of the terrible* (Isa 13:6-11).

• *Alas for the day! for **the day of the LORD** is at hand, and as a destruction from the Almighty shall it come* (Joel 1:15).

• *And the LORD shall utter his voice before his army: for his camp is very great: for he is strong that executeth his word: for **the day of the LORD** is great and very terrible; and who can abide it* (Joel 2:11)?

• *Woe unto you that desire **the day of the LORD**! to what end is it for you? **the day of the LORD** is darkness, and not light. As if a man did flee from a lion, and a bear met him; or went into the house, and leaned his hand on the wall, and a serpent bit him. Shall not **the***

12

day of the LORD *be darkness, and not light? even very dark, and no brightness in it* (Amos 5:18-20)?

- For ***the day of the LORD*** *is near upon all the heathen: as thou hast done, it shall be done unto thee: thy reward shall return upon thine own head.* (Oba 15).

*Hold thy peace at the presence of the Lord GOD: for **the day of the LORD** is at hand: for the LORD hath prepared a sacrifice, he hath bid his guests* (Zeph 1:7).

- ***The great day of the LORD*** *is near, it is near, and hasteth greatly, even the voice of **the day of the LORD**: the mighty man shall cry there bitterly* (Zeph 1:14).

- *Behold, **the day of the LORD** cometh, and thy spoil shall be divided in the midst of thee. For I will gather all nations against Jerusalem to battle; and the city shall be taken, and the houses rifled, and the women ravished; and half of the city shall go forth into captivity, and the residue of the people shall not be cut off from the city. Then shall the LORD go forth, and fight against those nations, as when he fought in the day of battle. And his feet shall stand in that day upon the mount of Olives, which is before Jerusalem on the east, and the mount of Olives shall cleave in the midst thereof toward the east and toward the west, and there shall be a very great valley; and half of the mountain shall remove toward the north, and half of it toward the south* (Zech 14:1-4).

- *Behold, I will send you Elijah the prophet before the coming of **the great and dreadful day of the LORD*** (Mal 4:5).

- *For yourselves know perfectly that **the day of the Lord** so cometh as a thief in the night. For when they shall say, Peace and safety; then sudden destruction* *cometh upon them, as travail upon a woman with child; and they shall not escape* (1 Thess 5:2,3).

- *But **the day of the Lord** will come as a thief in the night; in the which the heavens shall pass away with a great noise, and the elements shall melt with fervent heat, the earth also and the works that are therein shall be burned up* (2 Pet 3:10).

3. A Time of God's Wrath and Indignation

- *Why do the heathen rage, and the people imagine a vain thing? The kings of the earth set themselves, and the rulers take counsel together, against the LORD, and against his anointed, saying, Let us break their bands asunder, and cast away their cords from us. He that sitteth in the heavens shall laugh: the LORD shall have them in derision. **Then shall he speak unto them in his wrath**, and **vex them in his sore displeasure**. Yet have I set my king upon my holy hill of Zion. I will declare the decree: the LORD hath said unto me, Thou art my Son; this day have I begotten thee. Ask of me, and I shall give thee the heathen for thine inheritance, and the uttermost parts of the earth for thy possession. Thou shalt break them with a rod of iron; thou shalt dash them in pieces like a potter's vessel. Be wise now therefore, O ye kings: be instructed, ye judges of the earth. Serve the LORD with fear, and rejoice with trembling. Kiss the Son, lest he be angry, and ye perish from the way, **when his wrath is kindled but a little**. Blessed are all they that put their trust in him* (Psa 2:1-12).

- *Thine hand shall find out all thine enemies: thy right hand shall find out those that hate thee. **Thou shalt make them as a fiery oven in the time of thine anger**: the LORD shall **swallow them up in his wrath**, and **the fire shall devour them**. **Their fruit shalt thou destroy*** *from the earth, and their seed* from among the children of men (Psa 21:8-10).

• *Therefore **I will shake the heavens, and the earth** shall remove out of her place, in **the wrath of the LORD of hosts**, and in **the day of his fierce anger.*** (Isa 13:13).

• *Come near, ye nations, to hear; and hearken, ye people: let the earth hear, and all that is therein; the world, and all things that come forth of it. **For the indignation of the LORD is upon all nations, and his fury upon all their armies**: he hath **utterly destroyed them**, he hath **delivered them to the slaughter. Their slain** also shall be cast out, and **their stink** shall come up out of their carcases, and **the mountains shall be melted with their blood.** And all **the host of heaven shall be dissolved**, and **the heavens shall be rolled together as a scroll: and all their host shall fall down**, as the leaf falleth off from the vine, and as a falling fig from the fig tree* (Isa 34:1-4).

• *But the LORD is the true God, he is the living God, and an everlasting king: at **his wrath the earth shall tremble, and the nations shall not be able to abide his indignation*** (Jer 10:10).

• *Therefore wait ye upon me, saith the LORD, until the day that **I rise up to the prey**: for **my determination is to gather the nations**, that I may assemble the kingdoms, **to pour upon them mine indignation**, even all **my fierce anger**: for **all the earth shall be devoured with the fire of my jealousy*** (Zeph 3:8).

• *For, behold, **the day cometh, that shall burn as an oven**; and all the proud, yea, and all that do wickedly, shall be stubble: and **the day that cometh shall burn them up**, saith the LORD of hosts, that it shall leave them*

15

neither root nor branch. But unto you that fear my name shall the Sun of righteousness arise with healing in his wings; and ye shall go forth, and grow up as calves of the stall (Mal 4:1,2).

● *And said to the mountains and rocks, Fall on us, and hide us from the face of him that sitteth on the throne, and from **the wrath of the Lamb**: For **the great day of his wrath is come**; and who shall be able to stand* (Rev 6:16,17)?

The Seven Year Tribulation is *one unit* composed of Seven Seals containing Seven Trumpets and Seven Vials. We will not go through any part of it. Thus, it is Chapter Six of Revelation (with the Seals) that the **wrath of the lamb begins** (Rev 5:9; 6:1), not in Chapter Eight or Nine (with the Trumpets) or Chapter Sixteen (with the Vials). Wrath intensifies in each of these latter two, but it does not begin with them.

● *The same shall drink of **the wine of the wrath of God, which is poured out without mixture** into the cup of his indignation; and he **shall be tormented with fire and brimstone** in the presence of the holy angels, and in the presence of the Lamb: **<u>And</u> the smoke of their torment** ascendeth up for ever and ever: and they have no rest day nor night, who worship the beast and his image, and whosoever receiveth the mark of his name* (Rev 14:10,11).

● *Who shall not fear thee, O Lord, and glorify thy name? for thou only art holy: for all nations shall come and worship before thee; for **thy judgments are made manifest*** (Rev 15:4).

● *And there were voices, and thunders, and lightnings; and there was a great earthquake, such as was not since men were upon the earth, so mighty an earthquake, and so great. And the great city was divided* *into three parts, and the cities of the nations fell: and great Babylon came in remembrance before God, to give unto her **the cup of the wine of the fierceness of his wrath**. And every island fled away, and the mountains were not found. And there fell upon men a great hail out of heaven, every stone about the weight of a talent: and men blasphemed God because of the plague of the hail; for the plague thereof was exceeding great* (Rev 16:18-21).

B. Purposes of the Tribulation

1. To Prepare Israel for Her Messiah

• ***When thou art in tribulation**, and all these things are come upon thee, even in the latter days, **if thou turn to the LORD thy God**, and shalt be obedient unto his voice; (For the LORD thy God is a merciful God;) he will not forsake thee, neither destroy thee, nor forget the covenant of thy fathers which he sware unto them* (Deut 4:30,31).

• ***Come, my people**, enter thou into thy chambers, and shut thy doors about thee: hide thyself as it were for a little moment, **until the indignation be overpast*** (Isa 26:20).

• *Alas! for that day is great, so that none is like it: it is even **the time of Jacob's trouble, but he shall be saved out of it*** (Jer 30:7).

• *And I will bring you out from the people, and will gather you out of the countries wherein ye are scattered, with a mighty hand, and with a stretched out arm, and with fury poured out. And I will bring you into the wilderness of the people, and **there will I plead with you** face to face. Like as I pleaded with your fathers in the wilderness of the land of Egypt, **so will I plead with you**, saith the Lord GOD* (Ezek 20: 34-36).

17

• *And it shall come to pass in that day, that I will seek to destroy all the nations that come against Jerusalem. And I will pour upon the house of David, and upon the inhabitants of Jerusalem, the spirit of grace and of supplications: and **they shall look upon me whom they have pierced**, and they shall mourn for him, as one mourneth for his only son, and shall be in bitterness for him, as one that is in bitterness for his firstborn* (Zech 12:9,10).

• *And **I will bring the third part through the fire**, and will **refine** them as silver is refined, and will **try** them as gold is tried: **they shall call on my name**, and I will hear them: I will say, It is my people: and they shall say, The LORD is my God* (Zech 13:9).

• *Behold, he cometh with clouds; and every eye shall see him, and **they also which pierced him**: and all kindreds of the earth shall wail because of him. Even so, Amen* (Rev 1:7).

2. To Punish the World

• *And **I will punish the world for their evil**, and **the wicked** for their iniquity; and I will cause the arrogancy of **the proud** to cease, and will lay low the haughtiness of **the terrible*** (Isa 13:11).

• *With my soul have I desired thee in the night; yea, with my spirit within me will I seek thee early: for **when thy judgments are in the earth**, the **inhabitants of the world** will learn righteousness* (Isa 26:9). • *For, behold, the LORD cometh out of his place **to punish the inhabitants of the earth** for their iniquity: the earth also shall disclose her blood, and shall no more cover her slain* (Isa 26:21).

• *Thus saith the LORD of hosts, Behold, **evil shall go forth from nation to nation**, and a great whirlwind* *shall be raised up **from the coasts of the earth**. And the slain of the LORD shall be at that day **from one end of the earth even unto the other end of the earth**: they shall not be lamented, neither gathered, nor buried; they shall be dung upon the ground* (Jer 25:32, 33).

There will still be mercy during these awful days. God does not leave Himself without a witness. While there is no mention of the Church being present to carry the Gospel message, we do read about the 144,000 (Rev 7), the Two Witnesses (Rev 11), and even angelic evangelists (Rev 14). That God in those days is still *willing that none should perish* (2 Pet 3:9) is seen in the *great multitude which no man could number of all nations...which came out of great tribulation* (Rev 7:9,14). As Revelation 6-18 chronicles the Tribulation with its three-fold series of judgements (the seals, trumpets, and vials); at the beginning, in chapter 6, we are given notice that **the great day of his wrath is come**. Thus from beginning to end, the Tribulation is the wrath of God. With these "final calls" there is for a while some mingling and mixture in the wrath; but from chapter 14 this will all cease, and we read only of *the wine of the wrath of God which is poured out **without mixture*** (14:10).

C. Timing of the Tribulation

1. It is Connected with the Return of Christ

Many of the above passages speak of the Lord's Return in their immediate context. Therefore the Second Coming of Christ is in direct proximity with this time of tribulation. The chronology of the seals, trumpets and vials in Revelation 6-18 demonstrates that only a short period of time is involved. Attempts fail that seek to detach the Tribulation events from the Second Coming and place them in past history.

• *Immediately after the tribulation of those days shall the sun be darkened, and the moon shall not give her light, and the stars shall fall from heaven, and the powers of the heavens shall be shaken: And **then shall appear the sign of the Son of man** in heaven: and then shall all the tribes of the earth mourn, and **they shall see the Son of man coming** in the clouds of heaven with power and great glory* (Matt 24:29,30).

2. Its Duration will be Seven Years

Virtually all Bible believing students, whatever their views, acknowledge that the first 69 weeks of Daniel's 70-week prophecy (Dan. 9:24-27) were fulfilled literally. That is: there would be 69 weeks of years (483 years) from the decree (contrary to popular opinion, this is likely to be that of Cyrus rather than Artaxerxes Longimanus!) to just before Christ's death. As the previous 69 weeks were literal weeks of years, so the 70th week will also be literal, and will therefore have a duration of seven years. That these Seventy Weeks are God's clock in His dealings with Israel is clear from the following.

• *Seventy weeks are determined upon thy people and upon thy holy city, to finish the transgression, and to make an end of sins, and to make reconciliation for iniquity, and to bring in everlasting righteousness, and to seal up the vision and prophecy, and to anoint the most Holy* (Dan 9:24).

That there is a gap between the 69th and 70th weeks is shown by the death of Christ and the destruction of Jerusalem taking place after the 69th but before the 70th week. This gap is the time in which Israel as far as God's open dealings are concerned has been set aside (Matt 23:37-39), and the Church becomes the primary focus. The gap covers the period of Israel's rejection of her Messiah.

• *And **after threescore and two weeks*** *(to which the seven weeks or 49 years covering the final portion of OT history are added)* ***shall Messiah be cut off****, but not for himself: and the people of the prince that shall come* ***shall destroy the city*** *and the sanctuary; and the end thereof shall be with a flood, and unto the end of the war desolations are determined* (Dan 9:26).

The *people of the prince that shall come* were the Romans under Titus who destroyed Jerusalem in AD 70. The *prince that shall come* is the Antichrist, and is here described as having his roots in the Roman Empire. He is described in the previous two chapters of Daniel as *the little horn* and having his origin from the same source. The 70th and final week begins when the Antichrist makes (*confirms*) a seven-year covenant with Israel. Compare, ***your covenant with death*** in Isaiah 28:15. The "many" in the following passage likely refers to other nations involved with this covenant.

• *And he shall confirm the covenant with many for* ***one week****: and in* ***the midst of the week*** *he shall cause the sacrifice and the oblation to cease, and for the overspreading of abominations he shall make it desolate, even until the consummation, and that determined shall be poured upon the desolate* (Dan 9:27).

Thus the final 70th week is divided into two halves. In the chronicling of the Tribulation in Rev. 6-18, frequent mention is made of these halves, and in fact the second half is described as ***times, time and half a time***; ***42 months***; and *1260 days*. Scripture refers to this as a *short work*.

• *Esaias also crieth concerning Israel, Though the number of the children of Israel be as the sand of the sea, a remnant shall be saved: For he will finish the work, and cut it short in righteousness: because **a short work will the Lord make upon the earth**.* (Rom 9:27,28).

D. Reality of the Tribulation

The designations, purposes and timing of the Tribulation could not be more clearly stated in the Bible. To spiritualize, symbolize or somehow attempt to apply these passages to history implies that the student for whatever reason is unwilling to face the reality of the words written. These days will come just as stated.

> • *Seek ye out of the book of the LORD, and read:* **no one of these shall fail**, *none shall want her mate: for my mouth it hath commanded, and his spirit it hath gathered them* (Isa 34:16).

At this point we should emphasize that it is not *a pick and choose* matter as to which portions of the Scriptures we take literally. The entire Bible throughout its sixty-six books is to be taken literally. When symbolic language is used it is only to heighten and illustrate literal truth. Symbols in the Bible never symbolize symbols! The prophecies of Christ's First Coming, and the events surrounding that Coming were fulfilled literally. He was literally born in Bethlehem (Mic 5:2), literally sold for thirty pieces of silver (Zech 11:12), literally given vinegar on the Cross (Psa 69:21). We are therefore justified in fully expecting that His Second Coming and the events surrounding it likewise to be fulfilled literally. The coming seven-year Tribulation is a terrible reality.

The primary matter before us concerns the question as to whether believers during this Church age will have to go through the Tribulation. That is, in reading the many Tribulation passages, and Rev. 6-18 itself, do we find reference to Bible believing Local Churches being present on earth in those grim days? Certainly, a reading of the above does not indicate so. Nevertheless there is debate on this question. Some believe we will indeed have to go through all or nearly all of this time of trouble. Others say we will go through half or part of the Tribulation. And still others maintain that we shall not so much as see a single day of that terrible time and will be taken away before it begins. This latter is, we believe, the correct view.

These three groups are known respectively as Post-tribulationists, Mid-tribulationists, and Pre-tribulationists. Another recent group known as "pre-wrath", teaches that believers will go through most of the Tribulation but will be raptured just before the vials described in Revelation 16 are poured out. While the greater number of premillennialists are pretribulational, in recent years and especially on the Internet argument against this position has increased.

It needs to be remembered that each of these groups is <u>Pre</u>-millennial. That is, each believes that Christ will literally return to reign on the earth. This is in stark contrast to the <u>A</u>-millennialists, who, as they do not interpret the prophetic Scriptures literally, are able to deny that there will even be a seven-year Tribulation or a thousand-year reign of Christ upon the earth. Also the <u>Post</u>-millennialists (heard from very little these days) take the same non-literal view of Bible prophecy and teach that through the preaching of the Gospel the world will become Christianized and then Christ will return.

The following Scriptural evidence appears to be conclusive that believers will, as 1 Thessalonians 1:10 states so clearly, be *delivered from the wrath to come.* The Scriptures show clearly that the purposes of the Tribulation are not for the one who has placed faith in the finished work of the Lord Jesus Christ upon the Cross. Wrath fell on Him, it will not fall on us (or near us). *It is FINISHED.* John 19:30, is in fact the primary basis of the pretribulational Rapture.

CHAPTER 2

The Rapture and Return Contrasted From Scripture

During the 1800s renewed interest was kindled in the Second Coming of Christ. Many began to break away from the Catholic and Reformed Church teaching that the Old Testament promises to Israel are fulfilled in the Church (replacement theology), and that the Church in its growth fulfils prophecies concerning the millennium on earth. One simple means of exposing this error was merely to write out and categorise the many Scripture passages dealing with His Coming. An example of this exercise was the widely read book, *Jesus Is Coming* by William E. Blackstone. When all of the Scriptures are thus set out, and their differences noted and categorized, it becomes clear that there is indeed a Rapture that is to be distinguished from Christ's Return to earth; that there is a Tribulation and a literal reign of Christ from David's Throne upon earth; that, at the Rapture, Christ comes *for* His Church in the air; and that at His Return, He comes *with* His Church to the earth. The following sets out and distinguishes virtually all of the Scriptures dealing with these two phases of the Second Coming of Christ.

A. The Rapture of the Church

1. Believers Caught Up, Gathered, In Christ's Presence, Delivered from Wrath

- *Watch ye therefore, and pray always, that ye may be accounted worthy to* **escape all these things that shall come to pass**, *and to stand before the Son of man* (Lk 21:36).

• *Let not your heart be troubled: ye believe in God, believe also in me. In my Father's house are many mansions: if it were not so, I would have told you. I go to prepare a place for you. And if I go and prepare a place for you, **I will come again**, **and** receive you unto myself; that where I am, there ye may be also* (Jhn 14:1-3).

• *Much more then, being now justified by his blood, we shall be **saved from wrath** through him* (Rom 5:9).

• *Behold, I shew you **a mystery**; We shall not all sleep, but **we shall all be changed**, In a moment, in the twinkling of an eye, at the last trump: for the trumpet shall sound, and the dead shall be raised incorruptible, and we shall be changed* (1 Cor 15:51,52).

• *If by any means I might **attain unto the resurrection of the dead**. Not as though I had already attained, either were already perfect: but I follow after, if that I may apprehend that for which also I am **apprehended of Christ Jesus**. Brethren, I count not myself to have apprehended: but this one thing I do, forgetting those things which are behind, and reaching forth unto those things which are before, I press toward the mark for the prize of **the high calling** of God in Christ Jesus* (Phil 3:11-14).

• *For our conversation is in heaven; from whence also **we look for the Saviour**, the Lord Jesus Christ: Who **shall change our vile body**, that it may be fashioned like unto his glorious body, according to the working whereby he is able even to subdue all things unto himself* (Phil 3:20,21).

• ***When Christ, who is our life, shall appear**, then shall **ye also appear with him** in glory* (Col 3:4).

• *And to **wait for his Son** from heaven, whom he raised from the dead, even Jesus, which **delivered us from the wrath to come*** (1 Thess. 1:10).

• *For what is our hope, or joy, or crown of rejoicing? Are not even ye **in the presence** of our Lord Jesus Christ **at his coming*** (1 Thess 2:19)?

• *To the end he may **stablish your hearts unblameable in holiness** before God, even our Father, **at the coming** of our Lord Jesus Christ with all his saints* (1 Thess 3:13).

• *For this we say unto you by the word of the Lord, that we which are alive and **remain unto the coming** of the Lord shall not prevent them which are asleep. For the Lord himself **shall descend** from heaven with a shout, with the voice of the archangel, and with the trump of God: and the dead in Christ shall rise first: Then we which are alive and remain shall be **caught up together with them in the clouds**, to meet the Lord in the air: and so shall we ever be with the Lord. Wherefore comfort one another with these* words (1Thess 4:15-18).

• *But ye, brethren, are not in darkness, that that day should overtake you as a thief. Ye are all the children of light, and the children of the day: we are not of the night, nor of darkness. Therefore let us not sleep, as do others; but let us watch and be sober. For they that sleep sleep in the night; and they that be drunken are drunken in the night. But let us, who are of the day, be sober, putting on the breastplate of faith and love; and for an helmet, the hope of salvation. For **God hath not appointed us to wrath**, but to obtain salvation by our Lord Jesus Christ, Who died for us, that, whether we wake or sleep, **we should live together with him*** (1 Thess 5:4-10).

• *Seeing it is a righteous thing with God* **to recompense tribulation to them that trouble you***; And to you who are troubled rest with us, when the Lord Jesus* **shall be revealed from heaven** *with his mighty angels, In flaming fire taking vengeance on them that know not God, and that obey not the gospel of our Lord Jesus Christ: Who shall be punished with everlasting destruction from the presence of the Lord, and from the glory of his power;* **When he shall come to be glorified in his saints***, and to be admired in all them that believe (because our testimony among you was believed) in that day* (2 Thess 1:6-10). [While this verse is commonly thought to refer to the Return rather than the Rapture, it may in fact refer to the Rapture and the judgements He will *recompense* upon earth during the *Tribulation* (verse 6)].

• *Now we beseech you, brethren,* **by the coming** *of our Lord Jesus Christ, and* **by our gathering together unto him** (2 Thess 2:1).

• *And now* **ye know what withholdeth** *that he might be revealed in his time. For the mystery of iniquity doth already work: only* **he who now letteth will let, until he be taken out of the way.** *And then shall that Wicked be revealed, whom the Lord shall consume with the spirit of his mouth, and shall destroy with the brightness of his coming* (2 Thess 2:6-8). [Note: The Holy Spirit indwelt Church as salt and light is the hindering influence in the world today. The Holy Spirit as in Old Testament times will continue to work in conversion of sinners during the Tribulation].

• *But rejoice, inasmuch as ye are partakers of Christ's sufferings; that,* **when his glory shall be revealed***, ye may be glad also with exceeding joy* (1 Pet 4:13).

• *And when the chief Shepherd **shall appear, ye shall receive a crown of glory** that fadeth not away* (1 Pet 5:4).

• *Beloved, now are we the sons of God, and it doth not yet appear what we shall be: but we know that, **when he shall appear, we shall be like him**; for we shall see him as he is. And every man that hath this hope in him purifieth himself, even as he is pure* (1 Jhn 3:2,3).

• *Because thou hast kept the word of my patience, **I also will keep thee from the hour of temptation, which shall come upon all the world**, to try them that dwell upon the earth. **Behold, I come quickly**: hold that fast which thou hast, that no man **take thy crown*** (Rev 3:10,11). [Crowns will be given at the Judgement Seat of Christ, which is after the Rapture but before the Return].

• *After this I looked, and, behold, a door was opened in heaven: and the first voice which I heard was as it were of a trumpet talking with me; which said, **Come up hither**, and I will shew thee things which must be hereafter. And immediately I was in the spirit: and, behold, a throne was set in heaven, and one sat on the throne* (Rev 4:1-3). [After viewing the Church Age, John sees the *things hereafter*, i.e. the Tribulation from the vantage point of Heaven, thus, a picture of the Rapture].

• *And when he had taken the book, the four beasts and **four and twenty elders** fell down before the Lamb, having every one of them harps, and golden vials full of odours, which are the prayers of saints. And they sung a new song, saying, Thou art worthy to take the book, and to open the seals thereof: for thou wast slain, and hast redeemed us to God by thy blood out of every kindred, and tongue, and people, and nation; And hast made us unto our God kings and priests: and we shall reign on the earth* (Rev 5:8-10). [The twenty-four elders are likely to be representatives of the Church, and are thus seen in Heaven during the events of Rev 6-18].

● *Let us be glad and rejoice, and give honour to him: for the marriage of the Lamb is come, and **his wife hath made herself ready**. And to her was granted that she should be arrayed in fine linen, clean and white: for the fine linen is the righteousness of saints. And he saith unto me, Write, Blessed are they which are called unto the marriage supper of the Lamb. And he saith unto me, These are the true sayings of God* (Rev 19:7-9). [The Bride/Wife of Christ has been in Heaven during the Tribulation (Rev 6-18)].

2. Imminent Expectancy of Christ's Return

● *But when they persecute you in this city, flee ye into another: for verily I say unto you, Ye shall not have gone over the cities of Israel, **till the Son of man be come*** (Matt 10:23).

● *But know this, that if the goodman of the house had known in what watch the thief would come, he would have watched, and would not have suffered his house to be broken up. **Therefore be ye also ready: for in such an hour as ye think not the Son of man cometh*** (Matt 24:43,44).

● ***Watch therefore, for ye know neither the day nor the hour wherein the Son of man cometh*** (Matt 25:13).

● *For the Son of Man is as a man taking a far journey, who left his house, and gave authority to his servants, and to every man his work, and commanded the porter to **watch**. **Watch ye therefore: for ye know not when the master of the house cometh**, at even, or at midnight, or at the cockcrowing, or in the morning: Lest* *coming suddenly he find you sleeping. And **what I say unto you I say unto all, Watch*** (Mk 13:34-37).

• *Let your loins be girded about, and your lights burning; And ye yourselves like unto men that **wait** for their lord, when he will return from the wedding; that when he cometh and knocketh, they may open unto him immediately. Blessed are those servants, whom the lord when he cometh shall find **watching**: verily I say unto you, that he shall gird himself, and make them to sit down to meat, and will come forth and serve them. And if he shall come in the second watch, or come in the third watch, and find them so, blessed are those servants. And this know, that if the goodman of the house had known what hour the thief would come, he would have watched, and not have suffered his house to be broken through. Be ye therefore ready also: for **the Son of man cometh at an hour when ye think not**. Then Peter said unto him, Lord, speakest thou this parable unto us, or even to all? And the Lord said, Who then is that faithful and wise steward, whom his lord shall make ruler over his household, to give them their portion of meat in due season? Blessed is that servant, whom his lord when he cometh shall find so doing. Of a truth I say unto you, that he will make him ruler over all that he hath. But and if that servant say in his heart, **My lord delayeth his coming**; and shall begin to beat the menservants and maidens, and to eat and drink, and to be drunken; The lord of that servant will come in a day when he looketh not for him, and at an hour when he is not aware, and will cut him in sunder, and will appoint him his portion with the unbelievers* (Lk 12:35-46).

• *Nevertheless **when the Son of man cometh**, shall he find faith on the earth* (Lk 18:8)?

• *And he called his ten servants, and delivered them ten pounds, and said unto them,* **Occupy till I come** (Lk 19:13).

• *And he beheld them, and said, What is this then that is written,* **The stone which the builders rejected, the same is become the head of the corner?** *Whosoever shall fall upon that stone shall be broken; but on whomsoever it shall fall, it will grind him to powder* (Lk 20:17,18).

• *And* **there shall be signs** *in the sun, and in the moon, and in the stars; and upon the earth distress of nations, with perplexity; the sea and the waves roaring; Men's hearts failing them for fear, and for looking after those things which are coming on the earth: for the powers of heaven shall be shaken. And* **then shall they see the Son of man coming** *in a cloud with power and great glory* (Lk 21:25-27).

• **And when these things begin to come to pass, then look up, and lift up your heads; for your redemption draweth nigh.** *And he spake to them a parable; Behold the fig tree, and all the trees; When they now shoot forth, ye see and know of your own selves that summer is now nigh at hand. So likewise ye, when ye see these things come to pass, know ye that the kingdom of God is nigh at hand. Verily I say unto you, This generation shall not pass away, till all be fulfilled. Heaven and earth shall pass away: but my words shall not pass away. And take heed to yourselves, lest at any time your hearts be overcharged with surfeiting, and drunkenness, and cares of this life, and so that day come upon you unawares. For as a snare shall it come on all them that dwell on the face of the whole earth.* **Watch ye therefore, and pray always, that ye may be accounted** *worthy to escape all these things* *that shall come to pass, and to stand before the Son of man* (Lk 21:28-36).

• *So that ye come behind in no gift;* ***waiting for the coming of our Lord Jesus Christ:*** *Who shall also confirm you unto the end, that ye may be blameless in the day of our Lord Jesus Christ* (1 Cor 1:7,8).

• *Therefore judge nothing before the time,* ***until the Lord come***, *who both will bring to light the hidden things of darkness, and will make manifest the counsels of the hearts: and then shall every man have praise of God* (1 Cor 4:5).

• *If any man love not the Lord Jesus Christ, let him be Anathema* ***Maranatha*** (1 Cor 16:22).

• *Holding forth the word of life;* ***that I may rejoice in the day of Christ***, *that I have not run in vain, neither laboured in vain* (Phil 2:16).

• *Let your moderation be known unto all men.* ***The Lord is at hand*** (Phil 4:5).

• *And the Lord direct your hearts into the love of God, and into* ***the patient waiting for Christ*** (2 Thess 3:5).

• *That thou keep this commandment without spot, unrebukable,* ***until the appearing of our Lord Jesus Christ*** (1 Tim 6:14).

• *Henceforth there is laid up for me a crown of righteousness, which the Lord, the righteous judge, shall give me at that day: and not to me only, but* ***unto all them also that love his appearing*** (2 Tim 4:8).

• ***Looking for that blessed hope***, *and the glorious appearing of the great God and our Saviour Jesus Christ* (Titus 2:13).

• *So Christ was once offered to bear the sins of many; and* **unto them that look for him shall he appear the second time** *without sin unto salvation* (Heb 9:28).

• *Not forsaking the assembling of ourselves together, as the manner of some is; but exhorting one another: and so much the more,* **as ye see the day approaching** (Heb 10:25).

• *For ye have need of patience, that, after ye have done the will of God, ye might receive the promise. For* **yet a little while, and he that shall come will come**, *and will not tarry* (Heb 10:36,37).

• **Be patient therefore, brethren, unto the coming of the Lord.** *Behold, the husbandman waiteth for the precious fruit of the earth, and hath long patience for it, until he receive the early and latter rain. Be ye also patient; stablish your hearts: for* **the coming of the Lord draweth nigh**. *Grudge not one against another, brethren, lest ye be condemned: behold,* **the judge standeth before the door** (Jms 5:7-9).

• *Having your conversation honest among the Gentiles: that, whereas they speak against you as evildoers, they may by your good works, which they shall behold,* **glorify God in the day of visitation** (1 Pet 2:12).

• *But* **the end of all things is at hand**: *be ye therefore sober, and watch unto prayer* (1 Pet 4:7).

• *Wherefore, beloved,* **seeing that ye look for such things**, *be diligent that ye may be found of him in peace, without spot, and blameless* (2 Pet 3:14).

• *Repent; or else* **I will come unto thee quickly**, *and will fight against them with the sword of my mouth* (Rev 2:16).

• *But that which ye have already* **hold fast till I come** (Rev 2:25).

• *Remember therefore how thou hast received and heard, and hold fast, and repent.* **If therefore thou shalt not watch, I will come on thee as a thief***, and thou shalt not know what hour I will come upon thee* (Rev 3:3).

• **Behold, I come quickly***: blessed is he that keepeth the sayings of the prophecy of this book* (Rev 22:7).

• *And,* **behold, I come quickly***; and my reward is with me, to give every man according as his work shall be* (Rev 22:12).

• *He which testifieth these things saith,* **Surely I come quickly***. Amen. Even so, come, Lord Jesus* (Rev 22:20).

3. Allusions to the Rapture

• *But* **as the days of Noe were, so shall also the coming of the Son of man be***. For as in the days that were before the flood they were eating and drinking, marrying and giving in marriage, until the day that Noe entered into the ark, And* **knew not until the flood came***, and took them all away; so shall also the coming of the Son of man be. Then shall two be in the field; the* **one shall be taken, and the other left***. Two women shall be grinding at the mill; the* **one shall be taken, and the other left***.* **Watch** *therefore: for* **ye know not what hour your Lord doth come***. But know this, that if the goodman of the house had known in what watch the thief would come, he would have watched, and would not have suffered his house to be broken up. Therefore* **be ye also ready: for in such an** *hour as ye think not the Son of man cometh* (Matt 24:37-44).

• *And as it was in the days of Noe, so shall it be also in the days of the Son of man. They did eat, they drank, they married wives, they were given in marriage, until the day that Noe entered into the ark, and the flood came, and destroyed them all. Likewise also as it was in the days of Lot; they did eat, they drank, they bought, they sold, they planted, they builded; But the same day that Lot went out of Sodom it rained fire and brimstone from heaven, and destroyed them all. Even thus shall it be in the day when the Son of man is revealed. In that day, he which shall be upon the housetop, and his stuff in the house, let him not come down to take it away: and he that is in the field, let him likewise not return back. Remember Lot's wife. Whosoever shall seek to save his life shall lose it; and whosoever shall lose his life shall preserve it. I tell you, in that night there shall be two men in one bed; the one shall be taken, and the other shall be left. Two women shall be grinding together; the one shall be taken, and the other left. Two men shall be in the field; the one shall be taken, and the other left. And they answered and said unto him, Where, Lord? And he said unto them, Wheresoever the body is, thither will the eagles be gathered together* (Lk 17:26-37).

• *And Enoch walked with God after he begat Methuselah three hundred years, and begat sons and daughters: And all the days of Enoch were three hundred sixty and five years: And Enoch walked with God: and he was not; for God took him* (Gen 5:22-24).

• *By faith Enoch was translated that he should not see death; and was not found, because God had translated him: for before his translation he had this testimony, that he pleased God* (Heb 11:5).

• *And it came to pass, as they still went on, and talked, that, behold, there appeared a chariot of fire, and horses of fire, and parted them both asunder; and **Elijah went up by a whirlwind into heaven**....They sent therefore fifty men; and they sought three days, but **found him not*** (2 Kng 2:11,17).

B. The Return of Christ to Earth

1. From Genesis to Psalms

• *That then the LORD thy God will turn thy captivity, and have compassion upon thee, **and will return and gather thee from all the nations**, whither the LORD thy God hath scattered thee* (Deut 30:3).

• *For I know that my redeemer liveth, and that **he shall stand at the latter day upon the earth*** (Job 19:25).

• ***Yet have I set my king upon my holy hill of Zion**. I will declare the decree: the LORD hath said unto me, Thou art my Son; this day have I begotten thee. Ask of me, and I shall give thee the heathen for thine inheritance, and **the uttermost parts of the earth for thy possession**. Thou shalt break them with a rod of iron; thou shalt dash them in pieces like a potter's vessel* (Psa 2:6-9).

• *Then the earth shook and trembled; the foundations also of the hills moved and were shaken, because he was wroth. There went up a smoke out of his nostrils, and fire out of his mouth devoured: coals were kindled by it. He bowed the heavens also, **and came down**: and darkness was under his feet. And he rode upon a cherub, and did fly: yea, he did fly upon the wings of the wind. He made darkness his secret place; his pavilion round about him were dark waters and thick clouds of the skies. At the brightness that was before him* *his thick clouds passed, hail stones and coals of fire. The LORD also thundered in the heavens, and the Highest gave his voice; hail stones and coals of fire. Yea, he sent out his arrows, and scattered them; and he shot out lightnings, and discomfited them. Then the channels of waters were seen, and the foundations of the world were discovered at thy rebuke, O LORD, at the blast of the breath of thy nostrils.* **He sent from above, he took me, he drew me** *out of many waters.* **He delivered me** *from my strong enemy, and from them which hated me: for they were too strong for me* (Psa 18:7-17).

• *Lift up your heads, O ye gates; and be ye lift up, ye everlasting doors; and* **the King of glory shall come in**. *Who is this King of glory? The LORD strong and mighty, the LORD mighty in battle. Lift up your heads, O ye gates; even lift them up, ye everlasting doors; and* **the King of glory shall come in** (Psa 24:7-9).

• **Gird thy sword upon thy thigh, O most mighty**, *with thy glory and thy majesty. And in thy majesty ride prosperously because of truth and meekness and righteousness; and thy right hand shall teach thee terrible things. Thine arrows are sharp in the heart of the king's enemies; whereby the people fall under thee.* **Thy throne, O God**, *is for ever and ever: the sceptre of thy kingdom is a right sceptre* (Psa 45:3-6).

• *The heathen raged, the kingdoms were moved:* **he uttered his voice, the earth melted**. *The LORD of hosts is with us; the God of Jacob is our refuge. Selah. Come, behold the works of the LORD,* **what desolations he hath made in the earth**. *He maketh wars to cease unto the end of the earth; he breaketh the bow, and cutteth the spear in sunder; he burneth the chariot in the fire. Be still, and know that I am God:* **I will be exalted among the heathen, I will be exalted in the earth** (Psa 46:6-10).

• *For the LORD most high is terrible; he is **a*** ***great King over all the earth**. He shall subdue the people under us, and the nations under our feet. He shall choose our inheritance for us, the excellency of Jacob whom he loved. Selah. **God is gone up with a shout, the LORD with the sound of a trumpet** (Psa 47:2-5).*

• *The mighty God, even the LORD, hath spoken, and called the earth from the rising of the sun unto the going down thereof. Out of Zion, the perfection of beauty, God hath shined. **Our God shall come**, and shall not keep silence: a fire shall devour before him, and it shall be very tempestuous round about him. He shall call to the heavens from above, and to the earth, that he may judge his people. **Gather my saints together unto me**; those that have made a covenant with me by sacrifice (Psa 51:1-5).*

• *Say among the heathen that the LORD reigneth: the world also shall be established that it shall not be moved: he shall judge the people righteously. Let the heavens rejoice, and let the earth be glad; let the sea roar, and the fulness thereof. Let the field be joyful, and all that is therein: then shall all the trees of the wood rejoice Before the LORD: **for he cometh, for he cometh to judge the earth**: he shall judge the world with righteousness, and the people with his truth (Psa 96:10-13).*

• *The Lord at thy right hand **shall strike through kings in the day of his wrath** (Psa 110:5).*

• *Bow thy heavens, O LORD, and **come down**: touch the mountains, and they shall smoke. Cast forth lightning, and scatter them: shoot out thine arrows, and destroy them (Psa 144:5,6).*

2. From Isaiah to Daniel

• *For every battle of the warrior is with confused noise, and garments rolled in blood; but this shall be with burning and fuel of fire. For unto us a child is born, unto us a son is given: and **the government shall be upon his shoulder***: *and his name shall be called Wonderful, Counsellor, The mighty God, The everlasting Father, The Prince of Peace. **Of the increase of his government and peace there shall be no end, upon the throne of David, and upon his kingdom**, to order it, and to establish it with judgment and with justice from henceforth even for ever. The zeal of the LORD of hosts will perform this* (Isa 9:5-7).

• *And **there shall come forth a rod out of the stem of Jesse, and a Branch shall grow out of his roots**: And the spirit of the LORD shall rest upon him, the spirit of wisdom and understanding, the spirit of counsel and might, the spirit of knowledge and of the fear of the LORD; And shall make him of quick understanding in the fear of the LORD: and he shall not judge after the sight of his eyes, neither reprove after the hearing of his ears: But with righteousness shall he judge the poor, and reprove with equity for the meek of the earth: and **he shall smite the earth** with the rod of his mouth, and with the breath of his lips shall he slay the wicked* (Isa 11:1-4).

• ***The earth is utterly broken down**, the earth is clean **dissolved**, the earth is **moved** exceedingly. The earth shall **reel to and fro** like a drunkard, and shall be **removed** like a cottage; and the transgression thereof shall be heavy upon it; and it shall fall, and not rise again. And it shall come to pass **in that day, that the LORD shall punish the host of the high ones** that are on high, and the kings of the earth upon the earth. And they*

40

*shall be gathered together, as prisoners are gathered in the pit, and shall be shut up in the prison, and after many days shall they be visited. Then the moon shall be confounded, and the sun ashamed, when **the LORD of hosts shall reign in mount Zion, and in Jerusalem**, and before his ancients gloriously* (Isa 24:19-23).

• *And it shall be said in that day, Lo, this is our God; **we have waited for him**, and he will save us: this is the LORD; **we have waited for him**, we will be glad and rejoice in his salvation* (Isa 25:9).

• *And there shall be upon every high mountain, and upon every high hill, rivers and streams of waters in **the day of the great slaughter, when the towers fall**. Moreover the light of the moon shall be as the light of the sun, and the light of the sun shall be sevenfold, as the light of seven days, in the day that the LORD bindeth up the breach of his people, and healeth the stroke of their wound. Behold, **the name of the LORD cometh from far, burning with his anger**, and the burden thereof is heavy: his lips are full of indignation, and his tongue as a devouring fire: And his breath, as an overflowing stream, shall reach to the midst of the neck, to sift the nations with the sieve of vanity: and there shall be a bridle in the jaws of the people, causing them to err. Ye shall have a song, as in the night when a holy solemnity is kept; and gladness of heart, as when one goeth with a pipe to come into the mountain of the LORD, to the mighty One of Israel. And **the LORD shall cause his glorious voice to be heard**, and shall shew the lighting down of his arm, with the indignation of his anger, and with the flame of a devouring fire, with scattering, and tempest, and hailstones.* (Isa 30:25-30).

• *For thus hath the LORD spoken unto me, Like as the lion and the young lion roaring on his prey, when a multitude of shepherds is called forth against him, he* *will not be afraid of their voice, nor abase himself for the noise of them: so shall **the LORD of hosts come down to fight for mount Zion**, and for the hill thereof. As birds flying, **so will the LORD of hosts defend Jerusalem**; defending also he will deliver it; and passing over he will preserve it* (Isa 31:4,5).

• *Say to them that are of a fearful heart, Be strong, fear not: behold, your God will come with vengeance, even God with a recompence; **he will come** and save you* (Isa 35:4).

• *Behold, **the Lord GOD will come** with strong hand, and his arm shall rule for him: behold, his reward is with him, and his work before him* (Isa 40:10).

• ***The LORD shall go forth as a mighty man**, he shall stir up jealousy like a man of war: he shall cry, yea, roar; he shall prevail against his enemies. I have long time holden my peace; I have been still, and refrained myself: now will I cry like a travailing woman; I will destroy and devour at once. I will make waste mountains and hills, and dry up all their herbs; and I will make the rivers islands, and I will dry up the pools. And I will bring the blind by a way that they knew not; I will lead them in paths that they have not known: I will make darkness light before them, and crooked things straight. These things will I do unto them, and not forsake them* (Isa 42:13-16).

• ***Arise, shine; for thy light is come, and the glory of the LORD is risen upon thee**. For, behold, the darkness shall cover the earth, and gross darkness the people: but **the LORD shall arise upon thee**, and his glory shall be seen upon thee. And the Gentiles shall come to thy light, and kings to the brightness of **thy rising*** (Isa 60:1-3).

• *Who is this that cometh from Edom,* **with dyed garments** *from Bozrah? this that is glorious in his apparel, travelling in the greatness of his strength? I that speak in righteousness, mighty to save.* **Wherefore art thou red in thine apparel,** *and thy garments like him that* **treadeth in the winefat?** *I have* **trodden the winepress alone;** *and of the people there was none with me: for* **I will tread them** *in mine anger, and* **trample them** *in my fury; and* **their blood shall be sprinkled upon my garments,** *and I will* **stain all my raiment.** *For the day of vengeance is in mine heart, and the year of my redeemed is come. And I looked, and there was none to help; and I wondered that there was none to uphold: therefore mine own arm brought salvation unto me; and my fury, it upheld me. And* **I will tread down the people in mine anger,** *and make them drunk in my fury, and I will bring down their strength to the earth* (Isa 63:1-6).

• *For, behold,* **the LORD will come with fire,** *and with his chariots like a whirlwind, to render his anger with fury, and his rebuke with flames of fire. For by fire and by his sword will the LORD plead with all flesh: and* **the slain of the LORD shall be many** (Isa 66:15,16).

• *Behold, the days come, saith the LORD, that* **I will raise unto David a righteous Branch,** *and* **a King shall reign and prosper,** *and shall execute judgment and justice in the earth. In his days Judah shall be saved, and Israel shall dwell safely: and this is his name whereby he shall be called, THE LORD OUR RIGHTEOUSNESS* (Jer 23:5,6).

• *Therefore prophesy thou against them all these words, and say unto them,* **The LORD shall roar from on high,** *and utter his voice from his holy habitation; he shall mightily roar upon his habitation; he shall give a shout, as they that tread the grapes, against all the* *inhabitants of the earth. A noise shall come even to the ends of the earth; for **the LORD hath a controversy with the nations**, he will plead with all flesh; he will give them that are wicked to the sword, saith the LORD* (Jer 25:30,31).

• *Behold, **the whirlwind of the LORD goeth forth with fury**, a continuing whirlwind: it shall fall with pain upon the head of the wicked. The fierce anger of the LORD shall not return, until he hath done it, and until he have performed the intents of his heart: **in the latter days ye shall consider it*** (Jer 30:23,24).

• *As I live, saith the Lord GOD, surely with a mighty hand, and with a stretched out arm, and with fury poured out, will I rule over you. And **I will bring you out from the people,** and will gather you out of the countries wherein ye are scattered, with a mighty hand, and with a stretched out arm, and with fury poured out. And **I will bring you into the wilderness of the people,** and there will I plead with you face to face* (Ezek 20:33-35).

• *Thus saith the Lord GOD; Remove the diadem, and take off the crown: this shall not be the same: exalt him that is low, and abase him that is high. **I will overturn, overturn, overturn, it: and it shall be no more, until he come whose right it is; and I will give it him*** (Ezek 21:26,27).

• *So that the fishes of the sea, and the fowls of the heaven, and the beasts of the field, and all creeping things that creep upon the earth, and **all the men that are upon the face of the earth, shall shake at my presence**, and the mountains shall be thrown down, and the steep places shall fall, and every wall shall fall to the ground. And I will call for a sword against him throughout all my mountains, saith the Lord GOD: every man's sword shall be against his brother. And I will plead against him with* *pestilence and with blood; and I will rain upon him, and upon his bands, and upon the many people that are with him, an overflowing rain, and great hailstones, fire, and brimstone. Thus will I magnify myself, and sanctify myself; and I will be known in the eyes of many nations, and they shall know that I am the LORD* (Ezek 38:20-23).

• *And, behold, **the glory of the God of Israel came from the way of the east: and his voice was like a noise of many waters: and the earth shined with his glory**. And it was according to the appearance of the vision which I saw, even according to the vision that I saw when I came to destroy the city: and the visions were like the vision that I saw by the river Chebar; and I fell upon my face. And the glory of the LORD came into the house by the way of the gate whose prospect is toward the east. So the spirit took me up, and brought me into the inner court; and, behold, the glory of the LORD filled the house. And I heard him speaking unto me out of the house; and the man stood by me. And he said unto me, Son of man, **the place of my throne, and the place of the soles of my feet, where I will dwell in the midst of the children of Israel for ever**, and my holy name, shall the house of Israel no more defile, neither they, nor their kings, by their whoredom, nor by the carcases of their kings in their high places* (Ezek 43:2-7).

• *Then was the iron, the clay, the brass, the silver, and the gold, broken to pieces together, and became like the chaff of the summer threshingfloors; and the wind carried them away, that no place was found for them: and **the stone that smote the image became a great mountain, and filled the whole earth*** (Dan 2:35).

• *And **in the days of these kings shall the God of heaven set up a kingdom**, which shall never be destroyed: and the kingdom shall not be left to other* *people, but it shall break in pieces and consume all these kingdoms, and it shall stand for ever. Forasmuch as thou sawest **that the stone was cut out of the mountain without hands**, and that it brake in pieces the iron, the brass, the clay, the silver, and the gold; the great God hath made known to the king what shall come to pass hereafter: and the dream is certain, and the interpretation thereof sure* (Dan 2:44,45).

● *I saw in the night visions, and, behold, **one like the Son of man came with the clouds of heaven, and came to the Ancient of days, and they brought him near before him. And there was given him dominion, and glory, and a kingdom, that all people, nations, and languages, should serve him**: his dominion is an everlasting dominion, which shall not pass away, and his kingdom that which shall not be **destroyed*** (Dan 7:13,14).

● *And in the latter time of their kingdom, when the transgressors are come to the full, a king of fierce countenance, and understanding dark sentences, shall stand up. And his power shall be mighty, but not by his own power: and he shall destroy wonderfully, and shall prosper, and practise, and shall destroy the mighty and the holy people.   And through his policy also he shall cause craft to prosper in his hand; and he shall magnify himself in his heart, and by peace shall destroy many**: he shall also stand up against the Prince of princes; but he shall be broken without hand*** (Dan 8:23-25).

3. From Hosea to Malachi

● ***After two days will he revive us: in the third day he will raise us up, and we shall live in his sight****. Then shall we know, if we follow on to know the LORD: **his going forth** is prepared as the morning; and **he shall come** unto us as the rain, as the latter and former rain unto the earth* (Hos 6:2,3).

46

• *They shall walk after the LORD:* **he shall roar like a lion***: when he shall roar, then the children shall tremble from the west* (Hos 11:10).

• *Let the heathen be wakened, and come up to the valley of Jehoshaphat: for* **there will I sit to judge all the heathen** *round about. Put ye in the sickle, for the harvest is ripe: come, get you down; for the press is full, the fats overflow; for their wickedness is great. Multitudes, multitudes in the valley of decision: for* **the day of the LORD is near in the valley of decision***. The sun and the moon shall be darkened, and the stars shall withdraw their shining.* **The LORD also shall roar out of Zion***, and utter his voice from Jerusalem; and the heavens and the earth shall shake: but the LORD will be the hope of his people, and the strength of the children of Israel. So shall ye know that I am the LORD your God dwelling in Zion, my holy mountain: then shall Jerusalem be holy, and there shall no strangers pass through her any more* (Joel 3:12-17).

• *For, behold,* **the LORD cometh forth out of his place***, and will come down, and tread upon the high places of the earth. And the mountains shall be molten under him, and the valleys shall be cleft, as wax before the fire, and as the waters that are poured down a steep place* (Micah 1:3,4).

• *The mountains quake at him, and the hills melt, and* **the earth is burned at his presence***, yea, the world, and all that dwell therein. Who can stand before his indignation? and who can abide in the fierceness of his anger? his fury is poured out like fire, and the rocks are thrown down by him* (Nah 1:5,6).

• *For thus saith the LORD of hosts; Yet once, it is a little while, and I will shake the heavens, and the earth, and the sea, and the dry land; And* **I will shake all** *nations, and the desire of all nations shall come: and I will fill this house with glory, saith the LORD of hosts* (Hag 2:6,7).

• *Be silent, O all flesh, before the LORD: for **he is raised up out of his holy habitation*** (Zech 2:13).

• *Thus saith the LORD; **I am returned unto Zion, and will dwell in the midst of Jerusalem**: and Jerusalem shall be called a city of truth; and the mountain of the LORD of hosts the holy mountain* (Zech 8:3).

• *And **the LORD shall be seen over them**, and his arrow shall go forth as the lightning: and the LORD God shall blow the trumpet, and shall go with whirlwinds of the south. The LORD of hosts shall defend them; and they shall devour, and subdue with sling stones; and they shall drink, and make a noise as through wine; and they shall be filled like bowls, and as the corners of the altar. And the LORD their God shall save them in that day as the flock of his people: for they shall be as the stones of a crown, lifted up as an ensign upon his land* (Zech 9:14-16).

• *Behold, **the day of the LORD cometh**, and thy spoil shall be divided in the midst of thee. For **I will gather all nations against Jerusalem to battle**; and the city shall be taken, and the houses rifled, and the women ravished; and half of the city shall go forth into captivity, and the residue of the people shall not be cut off from the city. **Then shall the LORD go forth, and fight against those nations, as when he fought in the day of battle. And his feet shall stand in that day upon the mount of Olives**, which is before Jerusalem on the east, and the mount of Olives shall cleave in the midst thereof toward the east and toward the west, and there shall be a very great valley; and half of the mountain shall remove toward the north, and half of it toward the south. And ye*

48

shall flee to the valley of the mountains; for the valley of the mountains shall reach unto Azal: yea, ye shall flee, like as ye fled from before the earthquake in the days of Uzziah king of Judah: **and the LORD my God shall come, and all the saints with thee.** *And it shall come to pass in that day, that the light shall not be clear, nor dark: But it shall be one day which shall be known to the LORD, not day, nor night: but it shall come to pass, that at evening time it shall be light. And it shall be in that day, that living waters shall go out from Jerusalem; half of them toward the former sea, and half of them toward the hinder sea: in summer and in winter shall it be. And* **the LORD shall be king over all the earth**: *in that day shall there be one LORD, and his name one* (Zech 14:1-9).

• *For, behold, the day cometh, that shall burn as an oven; and all the proud, yea, and all that do wickedly, shall be stubble: and the day that cometh shall burn them up, saith the LORD of hosts, that it shall leave them neither root nor branch. But unto you that fear my name* **shall the Sun of righteousness arise with healing in his wings**; *and ye shall go forth, and grow up as calves of the stall* (Mal 4:1,2).

4. From the Gospels and Acts

• *As therefore the tares are gathered and burned in the fire; so shall it be in the end of this world.* **The Son of man shall send forth his angels, and they shall gather out of his kingdom all things that offend,** *and them which do iniquity; And shall cast them into a furnace of fire: there shall be wailing and gnashing of teeth. Then shall the righteous shine forth as the sun in the kingdom of their Father. Who hath ears to hear, let him hear* (Matt 13:40-43).

• *For* **as the lightning cometh out of the east, and shineth even unto the west; so shall also the coming of the Son of man be**. *For wheresoever the carcase is, there will the eagles be gathered together. Immediately after the tribulation of those days shall the sun be darkened, and the moon shall not give her light, and the stars shall fall from heaven, and the powers of the heavens shall be shaken: And* **then shall appear the sign of the Son of man in heaven: and then shall all the tribes of the earth mourn, and they shall see the Son of man coming in the clouds of heaven** *with power and great glory. And he shall send his angels with a great sound of a trumpet, and they shall gather together his elect from the four winds, from one end of heaven to the other. Now learn a parable of the fig tree; When his branch is yet tender, and putteth forth leaves, ye know that summer is nigh:* **So likewise ye, when ye shall see all these things, know that it is near, even at the doors**. *Verily I say unto you, This generation shall not pass, till all these things be fulfilled* (Matt 24:27-34).

• **When the Son of man shall come in his glory**, *and all the holy angels with him, then shall he sit upon the throne of his glory: And before him shall be gathered all nations: and he shall separate them one from another, as a shepherd divideth his sheep from the goats* (Matt 25:31,32).

• *For* **as the lightning, that lighteneth out of the one part under heaven, shineth unto the other part under heaven; so shall also the Son of man be in his day** (Lk 17:24).

• *Repent ye therefore, and be converted, that your sins may be blotted out, when the times of refreshing shall come from the presence of the Lord. And* **he shall send Jesus Christ**, *which before was preached unto you:*

Whom the heaven must receive until the times of restitution of all things, which God hath spoken by the mouth of all his holy prophets since the world began (Acts 3:19-21).

• *Because he hath appointed a day, in the which* **he will judge the world in righteousness by that man whom he hath ordained***; whereof he hath given assurance unto all men, in that he hath raised him from the dead* (Acts 17:31).

5. From Romans to Revelation

• *For I would not, brethren, that ye should be ignorant of this mystery, lest ye should be wise in your own conceits; that blindness in part is happened to Israel, until the fulness of the Gentiles be come in. And so all Israel shall be saved: as it is written,* **There shall come out of Sion the Deliverer***, and shall turn away ungodliness from Jacob: For this is my covenant unto them, when I shall take away their sins* (Rom 11:25-27).

• *And that, knowing the time, that now it is high time to awake out of sleep: for* **now is our salvation nearer than when we believed***. The night is far spent, the day is at hand: let us therefore cast off the works of darkness, and let us put on the armour of light* (Rom 13:11,12).

• *I charge thee therefore before God, and* **the Lord Jesus Christ, who shall judge the quick and the dead at his appearing and his kingdom** (2 Tim 4:1).

• *Searching what, or what manner of time the Spirit of Christ which was in them did signify, when it testified beforehand the sufferings of Christ, and* **the glory that should follow** (1 Pet 1:11).

- *For we have not followed cunningly devised fables, when we made known unto you **the power and coming of our Lord Jesus Christ**, but were eyewitnesses of his majesty* (2 Pet 1:16).

- *And Enoch also, the seventh from Adam, prophesied of these, saying, Behold, **the Lord cometh with ten thousands of his saints**, To execute judgment upon all, and to convince all that are ungodly among them of all their ungodly deeds which they have ungodly committed, and of all their hard speeches which ungodly sinners have spoken against him* (Jude 14,15).

- ***Behold, he cometh with clouds; and every eye shall see him**, and they also which pierced him: and all kindreds of the earth shall wail because of him. Even so, Amen* (Rev 1:7).

- ***And I looked, and behold a white cloud, and upon the cloud one sat like unto the Son of man, having on his head a golden crown, and in his hand a sharp sickle**. And another angel came out of the temple, crying with a loud voice to him that sat on the cloud, Thrust in thy sickle, and reap: for the time is come for thee to reap; for the harvest of the earth is ripe. And he that sat on the cloud thrust in his sickle on the earth; and the earth was reaped. And another angel came out of the temple which is in heaven, he also having a sharp sickle. And another angel came out from the altar, which had power over fire; and cried with a loud cry to him that had the sharp sickle, saying, Thrust in thy sharp sickle, and gather the clusters of the vine of the earth; for her grapes are fully ripe. And the angel thrust in his sickle into the earth, **and gathered the vine of the earth, and cast it into the great winepress of the wrath of God**. And the winepress was trodden without the city, and blood came out of the* *winepress, even unto the horse bridles, by the space of a thousand and six hundred furlongs* (Rev 14:14-20).

 • ***Behold, I come as a thief.*** *Blessed is he that watcheth, and keepeth his garments, lest he walk naked, and they see his shame. And **he gathered them together into a place called in the Hebrew tongue Armageddon*** (Rev 16:15,16).

 • *And **I saw heaven opened, and behold a white horse; and he that sat upon him was called Faithful and True**, and in righteousness he doth judge and make war. His eyes were as a flame of fire, and on his head were many crowns; and he had a name written, that no man knew, but he himself. And he was clothed with a vesture dipped in blood: and his name is called The Word of God. And the armies which were in heaven followed him upon white horses, clothed in fine linen, white and clean. And out of his mouth goeth a sharp sword, that with it he should smite the nations: and he shall rule them with a rod of iron: and he treadeth the winepress of the fierceness and wrath of Almighty God. And he hath on his vesture and on his thigh a name written, KING OF KINGS, AND LORD OF LORDS.* And I saw an angel standing in the sun; and he cried with a loud voice, saying to all the fowls that fly in the midst of heaven, Come and gather yourselves together unto the supper of the great God; That ye may eat the flesh of kings, and the flesh of captains, and the flesh of mighty men, and the flesh of horses, and of them that sit on them, and the flesh of all men, both free and bond, both small and great. And I saw the beast, and the kings of the earth, and their armies, gathered together to make war against him that sat on the horse, and against his army. And the beast was taken, and with him the false prophet that wrought miracles before him, with which he deceived them that had received the mark of the beast, and them *that worshipped his image. These both were cast alive into a lake of fire burning with brimstone. **And the remnant were slain with the sword of him that sat upon the horse, which sword proceeded out of his mouth:** and all the fowls were filled with their flesh* (Rev 19:11-21).

The above sets out many of the passages in the Bible dealing with the Second Coming of Jesus Christ. There is a clear distinction in these passages between Christ coming *for* His Church at the Rapture, and Christ at His Return coming *with* His Church to fight the Battle of Armageddon and reign upon the earth. In addition, apart from Revelation 6-18 in its entirety, we have seen virtually all of the key passages that deal with the coming Tribulation. Again, as one compares and reads through these passages it clear that the Church is simply not on earth during this time. No instructions are given to a Church during the Tribulation . It cannot be overstated: The Church is mentioned *twenty-two times* in Revelation 1-3, but *not once* in Revelation 4-18.

CHAPTER 3
Reasons for the Pretribulation Rapture

A. Ten Basic Reasons

1. The Doctrine of Imminence: Christ may come at any moment. Believers are never told to look for something to happen before the Rapture. While we may see the foreshadowing of the Tribulation, we are never told to look first for the Antichrist, the Seal judgements, the Mark, the Temple, the 144,000, the Two Witnesses etc. The believer today looks for Christ not Antichrist (Titus 2:13).

2. To say that Christ will not or cannot come today, as the mid or post tribulationist must say, is a grievous and arrogant thing to say and places them in the category of the servant who said, *my Lord delayeth his coming* (Lk 12:45).

3. Why have so few post and mid tribulationists not built bomb shelters and "stocked up"? If they really believe it, why have most not taken extreme measures for the extreme days coming?

4. None of the New Testament passages dealing with the Tribulation mentions the church (Matt. 13:30; 39-42, 48-50; 24:15-31; 1 Thess. 1:9-10; 5:4-9; 2 Thess. 2:1-11; Rev. 4-18).

5. There are no "Tribulation Instructions" given to the Church in the Epistles and Revelation 2,3. Specific instructions are not given as to how to deal with the Antichrist, the Mark, the Seal judgements, Trumpets judgements and Vial judgements etc.

6. The Church is not mentioned in *the things which shall be hereafter* section of Revelation 4-19 (cp. Rev 1:19); whereas it is mentioned 22 times during *the things which are* section (Rev 2,3; cp.1:19). Note the absence of the oft repeated phrase *unto the churches* (Rev 2,3) in the identical statement in Revelation 13:9.

7. In an extended passage (Rev 7:9-17), there is no statement linking those saved in the Tribulation to the Church.

8. The unity of Daniel's Seventieth Week is clearly demonstrated in Scripture. By contrast, postribulationists and midtribulationists destroy the unity of Daniel's Seventieth Week and confuse Israel's program with that of the Church. The Seventy Weeks are specifically said to apply to Israel (Dan 9:24).

9. The Seven Year Tribulation is one unit composed of Seven Seals containing Seven Trumpets and Seven Vials. We will not go through any part of it. Thus, it is Chapter Six of Revelation (with the Seals) that *the wrath of the Lamb* begins (Rev 5:9; 6:1), not in Chapter Eight or Nine (with the Trumpets) or Chapter Sixteen (with the Vials). Wrath intensifies with the Trumpets and the Vials, but it does not begin with them. Believers of the Church age will not go through any part of it.

10. The believeing church is *not appointed to wrath* (Rom 5:9; 1Thess 5:9).

B. Fifty Reasons by John Walvoord

This virtually "standardized" and classic presentation (from the internet) appeared in Dr. Walvoord's book *The Rapture Question* (Zondervan, 1957). I have taken the liberty to enlarge and edit his presentation in a number of places.

1. Historical Argument

"**1.** Though some as shown in 2 Thessalonians 2 had sought to introduce posttribulationism into the Church, the imminency of the Lord's return, which is an essential doctrine of pretribulationism, was clearly taught and believed in the early Church.

2. The formalisation of pretribulational truth in the past two centuries does not mean that the doctrine is new or novel. Its development and elucidation from the Scriptures is similar to that of other major doctrines during the history of the Church. In the early 1800s many began to take Bible prophecy literally and break out of the mould that had existed since the 400s. Both Catholicism and the Reformers held to a replacement theology in which the church was said to take the place of Israel, that God was in fact finished with Israel as a nation, and that the Tribulation and Millennium were only in a general sense fulfilled throughout history. To them prophecies of the Tribulation and Millennium bore no immediate proximity to Christ's Return. However, the extent to which believers saw pretribulational truth during those long centuries is not the main point; the above passages show that it is not only in the Bible, but it is in the Bible substantially!

2. Interpretational Argument

3. Pretribulationism is the only view that allows for a literal interpretation of all Old and New Testament passages on the Great Tribulation.

4. Pretribulationism distinguishes clearly between Israel and the Church and their respective programs.

3. Nature of the Tribulation

5. Pretribulationism maintains the Scriptural distinction between the Seven Year Tribulation which occurs in direct proximity to Christ's Second Coming and tribulation in general throughout the Church Age (Jhn 16:33).

6. The Tribulation is properly interpreted by pretribulationists as a time of preparation for Israel's restoration (Deut 4:29,30; Jer 30:4-11). It is not the purpose of the Tribulation to prepare the Church for glory.

7. None of the Old Testament passages on the Tribulation mention the church (Deut 4:29,30; Jer 30:4-11; Dan 8:24-27; 12:1,2).

8. None of the New Testament passages on the Tribulation mention the church (Matt 13:30; 39-42, 48-50; 24:15-31; 1 Thess 1:9-10; 5:4-9; 2 Thess 2:1-11; Rev. 4-18).

9. In contrast to midtribulationism, the pretribulational view provides an adequate explanation for the beginning of the Tribulation in Revelation 6. Midtribulationism teaches that the Tribulation begins with the blowing of the seventh trumpet in Revelation 11. This is refuted by the events of chapter 6 and especially verse 17.

10. The proper distinction is maintained between the prophetic trumpets of Scripture by pretribulationism. There is no proper ground for the pivotal argument of midtribulationism that the seventh trumpet of Revelation is the last trumpet of

1 Corinthians 15:51,52. There is no established connection between the seventh trumpet of Revelation 11, the last trumpet of 1 Corinthians 15:52, and the trumpet of Matthew 24:31. They are three distinct events. [See below on The Last Trumpet].

11. The unity of Daniel's Seventieth Week is maintained by pretribulationists. By contrast, postribulationism and midtribulationists destroy the unity of Daniel's Seventieth Week and confuse Israel's program with that of the Church. The Seventy Weeks are specifically said to apply to Israel (Dan 9:24).

4. Nature of the Church

12. The Translation (Rapture) of the Church is never mentioned in any passage dealing with the Second Coming of Christ to earth after the Tribulation.

13. The church is *saved from wrath* (Rom 5:9). It is *not appointed to wrath*

(1 Thess 5:9). It is *delivered from the wrath to come* (1 Thess 1:10). The Church therefore cannot enter *the great day of his wrath* (Rev 6:17).

14. Likewise the Church will not be overtaken by the Day of the Lord (1 Thess 5:1-9), which includes the Tribulation.

15. Though the Rapture is a mystery and not specifically revealed until the Epistles (1 Cor 15:51,52), the possibility of a believer escaping the Tribulation is mentioned in the Gospels (Lk 21:28-36).

16. The church of Philadelphia was promised deliverance *from the hour of temptation, which shall come upon all the world, to try them that dwell upon the earth* (Rev 3:10).

17. It is characteristic of divine dealing to deliver believers before a divine judgment is inflicted on the world as illustrated in the deliverance of Noah, Lot, Rahab, and others (2 Pet 2:5-9).

18. At the time of the Translation of the Church, all believers go to the Father's house in heaven (Jhn 14:3) and do not (as postribulationists teach) immediately return to the earth after meeting Christ in the air.

19. Pretribulationism does not divide the body of Christ at the Rapture on a works principle. The teaching of a partial Rapture is based on the false doctrine that the Translation of the Church is a reward for good works. It is rather a climactic consummation of salvation by grace.

20. The Scriptures clearly teach that all, not part, of the church will be raptured at the Coming of Christ for the Church (1 Cor 15:51-52; 1 Thess 4:17).

21. As opposed to a view of a partial rapture, pretribulationism is founded on the definite teaching of Scripture that the death of Christ frees from all condemnation.

22. The Godly remnant of the Tribulation are Israelites and Gentiles converted in the Tribulation, not members of the Church as maintained by posttribulationists. The Church is not mentioned in Revelation 6-18.

23. The pretribulational view, as opposed to posttribulationism, does not confuse general terms like elect and saints, which apply to the saved of all ages, with specific terms like Church and those *in Christ*. These latter refer only to believers of this age.

5. Doctrine of Imminency

24. The pretribulational interpretation teaches that the coming of Christ is imminent. While events of the Tribulation may appear on the horizon as a foreshadowing, we are to look to no other event intervening before the Rapture. We are to look for Christ rather than Antichrist (Titus 2:13).

25. The exhortation to be comforted by the Coming of the Lord (1 Thess 4:18) is very significant in the pretribulational view, and is especially contradicted by the posttribulational. Rather than offering comfort the posttribulationist must instead warn the Church that she faces the Antichrist, the wrath of Satan, the mark, wars, famine, pestilence, and especially the unfolding and ever increasing wrath of God in the sevenfold seal, trumpet and vial judgements.

26. The exhortation to look for *the glorious appearing of Christ* (Titus 2:13) loses its significance if the Tribulation must intervene first. Believers in that case should look for the terrible events of Revelation 6-18.

27. The exhortation to purify ourselves in view of the Lord's return has most significance if His coming is imminent (1 Jhn 3:2,3).

28. The church is uniformly exhorted to look for the Coming of the Lord Himself, while believers in the Tribulation are directed to look for the events of that which must unfold before He returns.

6. The Work of the Holy Spirit

29. The Holy Spirit as the restrainer of evil cannot be taken out of the world unless the Church, which the Spirit indwells, is translated at the same time. The Tribulation cannot begin until this restraint is lifted.

30. The Holy Spirit as the restrainer who indwells the Church (1 Cor 3:16) must be taken out of the world before "the man of sin," who dominates the Tribulation period, can be revealed (2 Thess 2:6-8). Yet, though the Church as salt and light is gone (cp. Matt 5:13,16), the Holy Spirit in this time will continue to work in the conversion of sinners.

31. [The expression *except there come a falling away first, and that man of sin be revealed* (2 Thess 2:3) refers to the total apostasy that must occur on earth before the *Day of Christ* takes place (2 Thess 2:2). That this *Day of Christ* refers to His actual Return to earth and not the Rapture is shown by the verses immediately before (2 Thess 1:5-10)].

7. Necessity of an Interval Between the Rapture and the Return

32. According to 2 Corinthians 5:10, all believers of this age must appear before the judgment seat of Christ in heaven, an event never mentioned in the detailed accounts connected with the Second Coming of Christ to the earth.

33. If the twenty-four elders of Revelation 4:1-5:14 are representatives of the Church as many expositors believe, it would necessitate the Rapture of the Church before the Tribulation, and certainly before Christ's Return to earth.

34. The coming of Christ for His Bride must take place before the Second Coming in which He returns to earth with His Bride (Rev 19:7-10). This is in accord with the Jewish order in which the groom goes to the bride's house and takes her to his father's house for the wedding ceremony.

35. Tribulation saints are not translated at the Second Coming of Christ but carry on ordinary occupations such as farming and building houses. They will bear children during the Millennium (Isa 65:20-25). This would be impossible if the Translation had taken place at the time of the Second Coming to the earth, as posttribulationists teach.

36. The judgment of the Gentiles following the Second Coming (Matt 25:31-46) indicates that both saved and unsaved are still in their natural bodies. This would be impossible if the Translation had taken place at the Second Coming.

37. If the Translation took place in connection with the Second Coming to the earth, there would be no need of separating the sheep from the goats as described in Matthew 25:31-46. This separation would have taken place in the very act of the Translation itself.

38. The judgment of Israel (Ezek 20:34-38), which occurs subsequent to the Second Coming, would likewise be unnecessary if the saved had previously been separated from the unsaved by a Translation at the end of the Tribulation.

8. Contrasts Between the Rapture and the Second Coming

39. At the time of the Rapture the saints meet Christ in the air, while at the Second Coming Christ returns with His saints (Zech 14:5; Jude 14), and also to meet the Tribulation saints on earth.

40. At the time of the Rapture the Mount of Olives is unchanged, while at the Second Coming it divides and a valley is formed to the east of Jerusalem (Zech 14:4,5).

41. At the Rapture living saints are translated, while no saints are translated in connection with the Second Coming of Christ to the earth.

42. At the Rapture the saints go to heaven, while at the Second Coming the scene of activity is entirely on the earth.

43. At the time of the Rapture the world is unjudged and continues in sin, while at the Second Coming the world is judged and righteousness is established on the earth.

44. The Translation of the Church is pictured as a deliverance before the day of wrath, while the Second Coming is followed by the deliverance of those who have believed in Christ during the wrath of the Tribulation.

45. The Rapture is described as imminent, while the Second Coming is preceded by definite signs. We cannot know the time of the Rapture, whereas time indicators are given to Tribulation saints for the Lord's Return to earth.

46. The Translation of living believers is a truth revealed only in the New Testament, while the Second Coming with its attendant events is a prominent doctrine of both Testaments.

47. The Rapture concerns only the saved, while the Second Coming deals with both saved and unsaved (cp. Rev 1:7).

48. At the Rapture Satan is not bound, while at the Second Coming Satan is bound and cast into the abyss.

49. No unfulfilled prophecy stands between the Church and the Rapture, while many signs must be fulfilled before the Second Coming.

50. No passage dealing with the resurrection of saints at the Second Coming mentions translation of living saints at that time." *John Walvoord.*

C. Further Reasoning For The Pretribulational Rapture

1. The Rapture is Not Timed; The Return is Timed

A number of passages as Matthew 24:44 and 25:13 tell us that Christ's coming will be in *such an hour as ye think not*, and that *ye know neither the day nor the hour.* This is in striking contrast to the three and one half years (*time, times and half a time*; Rev 12:14; cp. Dan 7:25; 9:27) that will elapse from the time the Antichrist breaks his covenant with Israel until Christ Returns. The time of His Return will be marked further by –

• The Jews fleeing into the wilderness for 1260 days (Rev 12:6).

• The ministry of the Two Witnesses will last for 1260 days (Rev 12:3).

• Jerusalem will be trodden down for 42 months (Rev 12:2).

• The Antichrist will reign for 42 months (Rev 13:5).

A study of these *timed* passages will show that they all occur in the second half of Daniel's Seventieth Week (cp. with Dan 9:27). It is therefore clear that believers during the Tribulation will be able to count the days and months from Antichrist setting up his image in the Jewish temple unto the Return of Christ. Therefore the Matthew 24:44; 25:13 type of passage cannot refer to the Return, and though the Rapture being a mystery is not revealed fully until the Epistles (1 Cor 15:51,52), these Gospel passages must have the Rapture in view. This leads naturally to the next point.

2. The Rapture is Intimated in the Gospels

Some ask: Why is the Rapture not seen in the Olivet Discourse (Matt 24,25; Mk 13; Lk 21). But, as the above shows: It is! It is also seen in our *being gathered* to Christ and the Father's house in John 14:1-3, and in Luke 17 it is seen in the examples of Noah and Lot. Further, Luke 21:36 shows that it will be possible to escape the coming Tribulation days. And, in Matthew 24 and 25, after describing the Tribulation and Christ's return in glory (24:27-31), there are *seven illustrations to promote watchfulness*. These exhortations, without any reference to time, point to an imminent, *at any moment* return of Christ for the believer.

- The Fig Tree 24:32-35

- The Days of Noah 24:36-39.

- The One Taken, One Left 24:40,41

- The Faithful Householder 24:42-44

- The Wise Servant 24:25-51

- The Ten Virgins 25:1-13

- The Talents 25:14-30

These passages cannot apply primarily to Tribulation saints fleeing from Antichrist, for they are able to count the days from the Beast setting up his image in Jerusalem to Christ's Second Coming. They rather stress the imminency and unexpectedness of His coming as seen in the Rapture. Tribulation saints will know the hour. These are illustrations for those who must: *Watch therefore: for ye know not what hour your Lord doth come* (Matt 24:42). Thus the Rapture, as a mystery fully revealed in the Epistles (1 Cor 15:51,52), is alluded to in the Gospels.

3. The Rapture and the Last Trumpet

The trump of God at the Rapture (1 Thess 4:16) is called the last trump in

1 Corinthians 15:52. Some have said this refers to the last of the seven trumpets blown by angels toward the end of the Tribulation, in which each issues in a cataclysmic judgement (Rev 8:2; 11:15). Others, that it refers to Christ's Return immediately after the tribulation of those days (Matt 24:29), when *He shall send his angels with a great sound of a trumpet, and they shall gather together his elect from the four winds, from one end of heaven to the other* (24:31). Post-tribulationists appeal to one or the other of these as the trumpet that will be blown at the Rapture, thus indicating that the Church will go through all or most of the Tribulation.

In response there clearly seems to be a distinction between trumpets in the hands of angels and the trumpet of the Rapture which is specifically called the trump of God (1 Thess 4:16). Further, in this connection, if there is a last trumpet of God, there must also be a *first trumpet of God*. And, indeed there is.

> • *And the LORD said unto Moses, Go unto the people, and sanctify them to day and tomorrow, and let them wash their clothes, And be ready against the third day: for the third day* **the LORD will come down** *in the*

*sight of all the people upon mount Sinai. And thou shalt set bounds unto the people round about, saying, Take heed to yourselves, that ye go not up into the mount, or touch the border of it: whosoever toucheth the mount shall be surely put to death: There shall not an hand touch it, but he shall surely be stoned, or shot through; whether it be beast or man, it shall not live: **when the trumpet soundeth long**, they shall come up to the mount. And Moses went down from the mount unto the people, and sanctified the people; and they washed their clothes. And he said unto the people, Be ready against the third day: come not at your wives. And it came to pass on the third day in the morning, that there were thunders and lightnings, and a thick cloud upon the mount, and the voice of the trumpet exceeding loud; so that all the people that was in the camp trembled. And Moses brought forth the people out of the camp to meet with God; and they stood at the nether part of the mount. And mount Sinai was altogether on a smoke, because the LORD descended upon it in fire: and the smoke thereof ascended as the smoke of a furnace, and the whole mount quaked greatly. And **when the voice of the trumpet sounded long, and waxed louder and louder**, Moses spake, and God answered him by a voice. And **the LORD came down upon mount Sinai**, on the top of the mount: and the LORD called Moses up to the top of the mount; **and Moses went up** (Exod 19:10-20).*

What a tremendous Old Testament picture this is of the Rapture! It is associated with a trumpet, *the first trumpet*! While angels were present (Acts 7:53), the trumpet is not seen to be in their hands. It is the trumpet of God. Compare: Psalms 47:5, *God is gone up with a shout, the LORD with the sound of a trumpet*. There will be trumpets sounded by angels at the end of the Tribulation and also as Christ returns to earth, but these are shown to be the trumpets of angels. The trumpet of the Rapture is the trump of God, as none bearing this description is seen again in the Scriptures; this in 1 Corinthians 15:51,52 is called *the last trump*.

The last trump is also a military expression. In Roman warfare, guards were summoned to their posts at the sound of a trumpet. They were relieved of their watch by a second or last trumpet. So we as believers are called to our watch, and to await the Lord's Return (Acts 20:31; 1 Cor 16:13; Eph 6:18; Col 4:2; 1 Thess 5:6; 2 Tim 4:5; 1 Pet 4:7; Rev 3:2). Shortly we too will hear the last trump. Likewise in Old Testament and Roman times the last trumpet was blown to call the soldiers home (2 Sam 18:16; 20:22). Scripture describes the Christian life as a warfare (2 Tim 2:1-4). We are urged to fight the good fight of faith (1 Tim 6:12). Paul's closing testimony bore witness to this, as he spoke not only of death but primarily of the Lord's Return:

> • *I have fought a good fight, I have finished my course, I have kept the faith: Henceforth there is laid up for me a crown of righteousness, which the Lord, the righteous judge, shall give me at that day: and not to me only, but unto all them also that love his appearing* (2 Tim 4:7,8).

At the Rapture, after the long warfare, after the long watch, the last trump will beckon God's soldiers home. Many also see a connection here with the Jewish Feast of Trumpets (Lev 23). The ceremony of the seventh month is marked by a series of short trumpet blasts and concluded by a long blast called the *tekiah gedolah*, the great or last trump. In the seven-feast calendar, the Feast of Trumpets is pretribulational in nature. It occurs before the Day of Atonement, Israel's day of affliction and atonement which prefigures her national salvation at Christ's Return. (See: Renald Showers, *Maranatha Our Lord, Come!* Friends of Israel Publ.).

As the Rapture will occur shortly before the commencement of the Seventieth Week of Daniel (Dan 9:24-

27) this same trumpet may also be heard by Israel alerting them to that fact. Jewish people around the world will be made to know that the final stage of the long suspended program *determined upon thy people and upon thy holy city* (Dan 9:24) has now begun. Isaiah 27 elaborates upon the 70th Week and describes the purging of Israel's iniquity *in the day of the rough and east wind*. The entire 27th chapter encompasses the *Day of the Lord* and the *Time of Jacob's Trouble* (Jer 30:7). This great work of Israel's chastening and restoration is **announced by a trumpet!**

- *Seventy weeks are determined upon thy people and upon thy holy city, to finish the transgression, and to make an end of sins, and to make reconciliation for iniquity, and to bring in everlasting righteousness, and to seal up the vision and prophecy, and to anoint the most Holy* (Dan 9:24).

- *In that day the LORD with his sore and great and strong sword shall punish leviathan the piercing serpent, even leviathan that crooked serpent; and he shall slay the dragon that is in the sea* (Isa 27:1).

- *Or let him take hold of my strength, that he may make peace with me; and he shall make peace with me. He shall cause them that come of Jacob to take root: Israel shall blossom and bud, and fill the face of the world with fruit. Hath he smitten him, as he smote those that smote him? or is he slain according to the slaughter of them that are slain by him* (Isa 27:5-7)?

- *Hath he smitten him, as he smote those that smote him? or is he slain according to the slaughter of them that are slain by him? In measure, when it shooteth forth, thou wilt debate with it: he stayeth his rough wind in the day of the east wind. By this therefore shall the iniquity of Jacob be purged* (Isa 27:7-9).

● *And it shall come to pass* **in that day**, *that the LORD shall beat off from the channel of the river unto the stream of Egypt, and ye shall be gathered one by one, O ye children of Israel. And it shall come to pass* **in that day, that the great trumpet shall be blown**, *and they shall come which were ready to perish in the land of Assyria, and the outcasts in the land of Egypt, and shall worship the LORD in the holy mount at Jerusalem* (Isa 27:12,13). Compare also Joel 2:1,15; Zeph. 1:16; Zech. 9:14.

4. The *Day of Christ* in II Thessalonians 2

2:1 *Now we beseech you, brethren, by the coming of our Lord Jesus Christ, and by* **our gathering together unto him**, **2:2** *That ye be not soon shaken in mind, or be troubled, neither by spirit, nor by word, nor by letter as from us, as* **that the day of Christ is at hand**. *2:3 Let no man deceive you by any means: for* **that day shall not come, except there come a falling away first**, *and that man of sin be revealed, the son of perdition;*

Some point to 2 Thessalonians 2:2,3 as indicating that Antichrist would be revealed before the *Day of Christ.* As it has been assumed that the term *Day of Christ* refers to the Rapture rather than the Return this would mean that the Rapture would follow rather than precede the Tribulation. Pretribulationists in seeking to answer this have made things difficult for themselves by arguing that the modern version reading, *Day of the Lord* rather than *Day of Christ* is the correct reading.

Some have further compounded the matter by suggesting the phrase, *falling away* (2:3) could refer to the Rapture rather than the apostasy that will accompany Antichrist during the Tribulation. This second proposal gives an unnatural meaning to the Greek noun *apostasia* (lit. apostasy). The word is found once else in Acts 21:21 (*to forsake* Moses). The verb

70

form *aphistēmi* is used 15 times and in the same sense. The *apostasia* is the total and utter apostasy that will accompany the Man of Sin during the Tribulation.

Rather than go through these unwarranted contortions they should have noted that *Day of Christ* as used here is defined by the immediately preceding passage.

> • *Seeing it is a righteous thing with God to recompense tribulation to them that trouble you; And to you who are troubled rest with us, when **the Lord Jesus shall be revealed from heaven with his mighty angels, In flaming fire taking vengeance on them that know not God, and that obey not the gospel of our Lord Jesus Christ:** Who shall be punished with everlasting destruction from the presence of the Lord, and from the glory of his power; **When he shall come to be glorified in his saints,** and to be admired in all them that believe (because our testimony among you was believed) in that day* (2 Thess 1:6-10).

This is the Lord Jesus coming with His saints and in flaming fire and vengeance at Armageddon. It is not the Rapture. This day in which Christ is so revealed will not come **except there come a falling away first, and that man of sin be revealed** (2 Thess 2:3). Nor for the believer will this *apostasia* come, for they will first be **gathered together unto him** (2:1). Here as in 1 Thessalonians the Rapture is described before the Tribulation.

1 Thessalonians 4:13-18 comes *before* 1 Thessalonians 5:1-11!

Returning to the *Day of Christ* question. The term is found seven times.

> • *Who shall also confirm you unto the end, that ye may be blameless in **the day of our Lord Jesus Christ*** (I Cor 1:8).

71

- *To deliver such an one unto Satan for the destruction of the flesh, that the spirit may be saved in **the day of the Lord Jesus*** (1 Cor 5:5).

- *As also ye have acknowledged us in part, that we are your rejoicing, even as ye also are our's in **the day of the Lord Jesus*** (2 Cor 1:14).

- *Being confident of this very thing, that he which hath begun a good work in you will perform it until **the day of Jesus Christ*** (Phil 1:6).

- *That ye may approve things that are excellent; that ye may be sincere and without offence till **the day of Christ*** (Phil 1:10).

- *Holding forth the word of life; that I may rejoice in **the day of Christ**, that I have not run in vain, neither laboured in vain* (Phil 2:16).

- *That ye be not soon shaken in mind, or be troubled, neither by spirit, nor by word, nor by letter as from us, as that **the day of Christ** is at hand* (2 Thess 2:2).

Pretribulationists have generally distinguished *the Day of Christ* from *the Day of the Lord* and have said that the former refers entirely to the time of blessing at the Rapture. This however poses a problem when we come to the seventh and last reference (II Thess. 2:2). In a comment on 2 Thess 2:2, *The Scofield Reference Bible* says:

A.V. has "day of Christ" 2 Thess 2:2, incorrectly, for "day of the LORD" (Isa. 2:12; Rev 19:11-21). The "day of Christ" relates wholly to the reward and blessing of saints at His coming, as "day of the LORD" is connected with judgement.

On the contrary, the AV, Received Text and vast majority of Greek manuscripts are correct in reading *day of*

Christ in 2 Thessalonians 2:2. The modern version *day of the Lord* reading has far less support among the total number of Greek manuscripts. And while the blessing and reward aspect is emphasized in the previous usages, the fact that *day of Christ* in 2:2,3 clearly relates back to 1 Thessalonians 1:4-10 (and also 1 Thess 5:1-11), demonstrates that there is a clear wrath aspect in the term. To draw a sharp distinction between *the Day of Christ* and *the Day of the Lord* is unwarranted and both must be virtually synonymous. Christ *is the Lord* who comes for His Church; but He also opens the seals of wrath during the Tribulation, and returns to fight the Battle of Armageddon.

In the term *Day of Christ*, there is the blessing and reward phase, but also the wrath and Return phases. In Revelation 5,6 we clearly see the wrath phase. It is Christ who opens the seals unleashing the *wrath of God* upon the earth (5:9; 6:1). When these seals are opened there is no doubt among those on earth that they have entered **the great day of the wrath of the Lamb.**

> • *And the stars of heaven fell unto the earth, even as a fig tree casteth her untimely figs, when she is shaken of a mighty wind. And the heaven departed as a scroll when it is rolled together; and every mountain and island were moved out of their places. And the kings of the earth, and the great men, and the rich men, and the chief captains, and the mighty men, and every bondman, and every free man, hid themselves in the dens and in the rocks of the mountains; And said to the mountains and rocks, Fall on us, and hide us from the face of him that sitteth on the throne, and from* **the wrath of the Lamb***: For* **the great day of his wrath is come***; and who shall be able to stand* (Rev. 6:13-17)?

5. The Restated Events in II Thessalonians

The prophetic events of Second Thessalonians are presented in the context of what Paul had previously taught the Thessalonians in his visit and in the First Epistle.

- Believers will be *delivered from the wrath to come* (1 Thess 1:10).

- Christ will return *with all his saints* (1 Thess 3:13).

- The Rapture was described (1 Thess 4:13-18).

- The Tribulation was described (1 Thess 5:1-11).

Paul had spent only three weeks in Thessalonica (Acts 17:1-9), yet it is clear from the First Epistle and now what they are reminded of in the Second Epistle that in that short time he had thoroughly grounded them in the truths of the Second Coming. Here from the great Apostle is the principle that young believers are to be taught the basics of Bible Prophecy and to *love the Lord's Return* (2 Tim 4:8). The following points are now reinforced:

• Christ Will Return in Fiery Judgement

And...the Lord Jesus shall be revealed from heaven with his mighty angels, In flaming fire taking vengeance on them that know not God, and that obey not the gospel of our Lord Jesus Christ: Who shall be punished with everlasting destruction from the presence of the Lord, and from the glory of his power (2 Thess 1:7-9).

• A *Gathering* (the Rapture) Comes Before the Fiery Return

Now we beseech you, brethren, by the coming of our Lord Jesus Christ, and by our gathering together unto him, That ye be not soon shaken in mind, or be *troubled, neither by spirit, nor by word, nor by letter as from us, as **that the day of Christ is at hand*** (2 Thess 2:1,2).

• The Times of Antichrist Come Before Christ's Fiery Return

*Let no man deceive you by any means: for **that day shall not come, except there come a falling away first, and that man of sin be revealed**, the son of perdition; Who opposeth and exalteth himself above all that is called God, or that is worshipped; so that he as God sitteth in the temple of God, shewing himself that*

*he is God. **Remember ye not, that, when I was yet with you, I told you these things*** (2 Thess 2:3-5)?

• The Removal of the *Hinderer* (The Holy Spirit Indwelt Church) Before the Antichrist is Revealed and Before Christ Destroys Him in Fiery Judgement

And now ye know what withholdeth that he might be revealed in his time. *For the mystery of iniquity doth already work: only **he who now letteth will let, until he be taken out of the way. And then shall that Wicked be revealed**, whom the Lord shall consume with the spirit of his mouth, and shall **destroy with the brightness of his coming*** (2 Thess 2:6-8).

• Delusion for *Them*

*Even him, whose coming is after the working of Satan with all power and signs and lying wonders, And with all deceivableness of unrighteousness in **them** that perish; because **they** received not the love of the truth, that **they** might be saved. And for this cause God shall send **them** strong delusion, that **they** should believe a lie: That **they** all might be damned who believed not the* *truth, but had pleasure in unrighteousness* (2 Thess 2:9-12).

• Thanksgiving for *You*

But we are bound to give thanks alway to God for ***you****, brethren beloved of the Lord, because God hath from the beginning chosen* ***you*** *to salvation through sanctification of the Spirit and belief of the* ***truth****: Whereunto he called you by our gospel, to the obtaining of the glory of our Lord Jesus Christ* (2 Thess 2:13,14).

Because of erroneous letters sent to the Thessalonians and their severe trials, they were being led to believe that they were in the Tribulation. Second Thessalonians is a corrective for believers of all ages who face severe persecution. While the experience may be painful, it is not the time of wrath spoken of in the Bible. The very fact that the Thessalonians were told not to be *troubled* or *shaken in mind* (2:2), is a certain proof that believers will not have to face the time of Antichrist and the *Day of Christ* in its wrath sense.

6. A Posttribulational Rapture is Contradictory

If Christ raptures all believers at the end of the Tribulation and slays all who have taken the mark of the beast, who will then be left in mortal bodies to populate earth during the Millennium?

If at the end of the Tribulation believers rise to meet Christ in the air, does it not seem strange that we would immediately return with Him to the earth? How can we rise to meet one who is returning to fight a war? How in such a scenario are we to be clothed in white robes and seated on white horses?

How can *the time of Jacob's Trouble* (Jer 30:7) be the time of the Church's trouble? If as stated the Sixty-nine Weeks of Daniel's prophecy apply to Israel (Dan. 9:24), how can the Seventieth Week apply to the Church?

If the Church is present on earth during the Tribulation, why after being mentioned 22 times in Rev. 1-3 is it not mentioned once in chapters 6-18? Why in Rev. 2,3 do we repeatedly read *He that hath an ear let him hear what the Spirit sayeth unto the churches*, whereas in Revelation 13:9 it is only *If any man have an ear, let him hear*? If the Church is on earth, why is its voice so silent? Why, like the Two Witnesses or the 144,000, does it not seek to be *salt and light* (Matt 5:13,16)? How can it be so moribund?

7. Arguing For but Not Preparing For a Mid or Posttribulational Rapture

Given the extent to which the Bible describes the absolute terror of the coming Tribulation days, and given the clear demonstration that believers will be *kept from the hour of temptation which shall come upon all the world*, it is strange that numbers of believers argue so fervently for a place on earth during that time. As Todd Stranberg writes: "You would think the desire to go through the Tribulation would be as popular as the desire to jump into a pit filled with vipers and broken glass. As illogical as it may seem....Many Christians argue strongly for the right to suffer persecution at the hands of the Antichrist and the one world government."

For one striking reason this attitude is completely contradictory. Post, mid, and pre-wrath tribulationists are not seen making much in the way of preparation for the coming Tribulation! A scan of the Internet will show that they argue very passionately against pretribulationalism and for the right to live on earth during that time. BUT: Where are the blankets, the bottled water, the crates of canned food, electrical generators, underground bunkers, hideaways up in the hills etc.? Where is the urgency to stock up? Will they only start their survival preparations after the Tribulation begins? Their argument does not seem to go beyond the rhetorical. Have they really grasped the implications of what they teach!?

8. It is a Grievous Error to Say, "Christ Cannot Return Today."

There is and has always been a battle for the hearts and minds of professing Christians concerning the Second Coming of Jesus Christ. It seems that Satan has a number of "fall back positions." Ultimately these are designed to put the believer into the position described in Luke 12:45: *But and if that servant shall say in his heart,* **My lord delayeth his coming**.

Note the *Fall Back Positions* used to avoid the *Perhaps Today* Rapture:

(1) "Christ will not literally and physically return to the earth. His Coming is spiritual. He is already here. The prophetic Scriptures are to be taken symbolically. They refer to the spiritual struggles of the Church throughout history."

(2) "If one must believe in the Second Coming then by all means be an amillennialist. There is: No Millennium; No Tribulation; No Rapture. Let Christ return, but let there be only a general judgement with the saved going to Heaven and the lost going to Hell."

• Allow individual Jews to be saved, but reject any thought of Israel's national salvation in the Land of Israel at Christ's Return.

• Make the Church the recipient of the promises to Israel. In fact, replace Israel with the Church and call the Church the *New Israel* (replacement theology).

• Ignore the historical fact that the Church of the first three centuries was for the most part premillennial and believed in the *imminent* Return of Christ.

Such a teaching of course gives very little practical reality to the Blessed Hope. To treat the prophetic Scriptures in the way amillennialists do *is the height of arrogance*. Yet this view is very much in vogue today, particularly among reformed churches.

(3) "If on the other hand one comes to accept that the prophetic Scriptures are to be basically taken literally: that there is a Millennium, a Tribulation, a future for Israel, imminency must still be rejected." A Perhaps Today hope can be avoided by resorting to the following.

• Remove any possibility of Christ coming today by projecting the Rapture into at least the middle of the Tribulation, and more preferably to its end. Life can for the most part go on as normal, and 1 John 3:3 (as one example) will not be as essential: *And every man that hath this hope in him purifieth himself, even as he is pure.*

• Ignore the huge amount of Scripture that points to the pretribulational Rapture, and concentrate instead upon the foolish notion that this doctrine had its origin in a "vision" that a fifteen year old Irish girl, Margaret MacDonald had in 1830. (This claim was made in a book by Dave MacPherson in 1973)

• Make the claim that the pretribulation Rapture was part of Jesuit plot to undermine the Protestant and reformed faith.

• Attack the lives and writings of J.N. Darby and C.I. Scofield. Focus the attack especially against the 1917 Scofield Reference Bible. Scofield was wrong in his textual comments and the "gap theory", but otherwise the notes are sound and spiritual and have been a help *to millions*.

• Look for the opposite of Titus 2:13; look for Antichrist rather than Christ. Instead of *looking for the Blessed Hope*, look for the Beast to set up his image in Jerusalem.

• Ignore the historical fact that though they were enduring severe persecution and their statements were less than precise, the Church of the first three centuries did believe in the imminency of Christ's Return - an essential part of the pretribulational Return.

The above demonstrate that the Pretribulational Rapture is a clear Biblical truth drawn from Scripture. It is the natural conclusion of the Bible's prophetic statements. It is in harmony with its different facets and harmonizes with God's program for Israel, the Church and the nations. In contrast, insurmountable problems and contradictions are inherent within the mid, pre-wrath and posttribulational positions. The Pretribulational Rapture is the only system that allows for Jesus Christ to come for His Church TODAY!

In his 1857 book, *The Apocalypse*, Joseph Seiss closes with the following illustration.

"Fiction has painted the picture of a maiden whose lover left her for a voyage to the Holy Land, promising on his return to make her his beloved bride. Many told her that she would never see him again. But she believed his word, and evening by evening she went down to the lonely shore, and kindled there a beacon-light in sight of the roaring waves, to hail and welcome the returning ship which was to bring again her betrothed. And by that watchfire she took her stand each night, praying to the winds to hasten on the sluggish sails, that he who was everything to her might come. Even so that blessed Lord, who has loved us unto death, has gone away to the mysterious Holy Land of heaven, promising on his return to make us his happy and eternal Bride. Some say that he has gone forever, and that here we shall never see him more. But his last word was, *"Yea, I come quickly."* And on the dark and misty beach sloping out into the eternal sea, each true believer stands by the love-lit fire, looking, and waiting, and praying and hoping for the fulfilment of his word, in nothing gladder than in his pledge and promise, and calling ever from the soul of sacred love, "EVEN SO, COME, LORD JESUS."

And some of these nights, while the world is busy with its gay frivolities, and laughing at the maiden on the shore, a form shall rise over the surging waves, as once on Galilee, to vindicate forever all this watching and devotion and bring to the faithful and constant heart a joy, and glory, and triumph which never more shall end."

Blessed are those servants, whom the Lord when he cometh shall find watching. Luke 12:37

INDEX OF WORDS AND PHRASES

85

SCRIPTURE REFERENCES

BOOK REFERENCE	PAGE
Gen 5:22-24	36
Exod 19:10-20	67
Deut 4:29,30	58
Deut 4:30,31	17
Deut 30:3	37
2 Sam 18:16	68
2 Sam 20:22	68
2 Kng 2:11,17	37
Job 19:25	37
Psa 2:1-12	14
Psa 2:6-9	37
Psa 18:7-17	38
Psa 21:8-10	15
Psa 24:7-9	38
Psa 46:6-10	38
Psa 47:2-5	39
Psalms 47:5	67
Psa 51:1-5	39
Psa 69:21	22
Psa 96:10-13	39
Psa 110:5	39
Psa 144:5,6	39
Isa 2:12	12
Isa 9:5-7	40
Isa 11:1-4	40
Isa 11:9	9
Isa 13:6-11	12
Isa 13:11	18
Isa 13:13	15
Isa 24:19-23	41
Isa 25:9	41
Isa 26:9	18
Isa 26:20	17
Isa 26:21	18
Isa 27:1	69, 70

Isa 27:5-7	69
Isa 27:7-9	69
Isa 27:12,13	70
Isaiah 28:15	21
Isa 30:25-30	41
Isa 31:4,5	42
Isa 34:1-4	15
Isa 34:16	22
Isa 35:4	42
Isa 40:10	42
Isa 42:13-16	42
Isa 60:1-3	42
Isa 63:1-6	43
Isa 65:20-25	62
Isa 66:15,16	43
Jer 10:10	15
Jer 23:5,6	43
Jer 25:30,31	44
Jer 25:32, 33	19
Jer 30:4-11	58
Jer 30:7	17, 69, 76
Jer 30:23,24	44
Ezek 20:33-35	44
Ezek 20: 34-36	17
Ezek 20:34-38	62
Ezek 21:26,27	44
Ezek 38:20-23	45
Ezek 43:2-7	45
Dan 2:35	45
Dan 2:44,45	46
Dan 7:13,14	46
Dan 8:23-25	46
Dan 8:24-27	58
Dan 9:24	58
Dan 9:26	21
Dan 9:27	21, 65
Dan. 9:24-27	20
Dan 12:1	11
Dan 12:1,2	58
Hos 6:2,3	46
Hos 11:10	47
Joel 1:15	12

Joel 2:1,15	70
Joel 2:11	12
Joel 3:12-17	47
Amos 5:18-20	13
Oba 15	13
Micah 1:3,4	47
Mic 5:2	22
Nah 1:5,6	47
Zeph 1:7	13
Zeph 1:14	13
Zeph. 1:16	70
Zeph 3:8	15
Hag 2:6,7	48
Zech 2:13	48
Zech 8:3	48
Zech. 9:14	70
Zech 9:14-16	48
Zech 11:12	22
Zech 12:9,10	18
Zech 13:9	18
Zech 14:1-4	13
Zech 14:1-9	49
Zech 14:4,5	63
Zech 14:5	63
Mal 4:1,2	16, 49
Matt 5:13,16	61, 77
Matt 10:23	30
Matt 13:30; 39-42, 48-50	55, 58
Matt 13:40-43	49
Matt 13:48-50	55
Matt 23:37-39	20
Matt 24:27-31	65
Matt 24:29	66
Matt 24:31	66
Matt 24:31	58
Matt 24:15-31	55
Matt 24:25-51	65
Matt 24:32-35	65
Matt 24:36-39	65
Matt 24:40,41	65
Matt 24:27-34	50
Matt 24:29,30	20

Matt 24:37-44	36
Matt 24:42-44	65
Matt 24:43,44	30
Matt 24:44	64, 65
Matt 25:1-13	65
Matt 25:13	30
Matt 25:13	30, 64, 65
Matt 25:14-30	65
Matt 25:31,32	50
Matt 25:31-46	62
Matt 39-42	55
Mk 13:19	11
Mk 13:34-37	31
Lk 12:45	55
Lk 12:45	78
Lk 12:35-46	31
Lk 17:24	50
Lk 17:26-37	36
Lk 18:8	31
Lk 19:13	32
Lk 20:17,18	32
Lk 21:25-27	32
Lk 21:36	25
Lk 21:28,36	59
24:15-31	55, 58
Jhn 14:1-3	26
Jhn 14:3	59
Jhn 16:33	57
John 19:30	23
Acts 1:11	9
Acts 3:19-21	51
Acts 7:53	67
Acts 17:1-9	74
Acts 17:31	51
Acts 20:31	68
Acts 21:21	70
Rom 5:9	26, 56, 59
Rom 9:27,28	21
Rom 11:25-27	51
Rom 13:11,12	51
1 Cor 1:7,8	33
I Cor 1:8	71

1 Cor 3:16	61
1 Cor 4:5	33
1 Cor 5:5	72
1 Cor 15:51,52	26
1 Cor 15:52	58, 66
1 Cor 16:13	68
1 Cor 16:22	33
2 Cor 1:14	72
Eph 6:18	68
Phil 1:6	68
Phil 1:10	72
Phil 2:16	33, 72
Phil 3:11-14	26
Phil 3:20,21	26
Phil 4:5	33
Col 3:4	26
Col 4:2	68
1 Thess. 1:9-10	55
1 Thess 1:10	59
1 Thess 1:10	23
1 Thess 2:19	27
1 Thess 3:13	27
1 Thessalonians 1:4-10	73
1 Thess 4:13-18	74
1 Thess 4:13-18	71
1Thess 4:15-18	27
1 Thess 4:16	66
1 Thess 4:17	60
1 Thess 4:18	60
1 Thess 5:1-9	59
1 Thess 5:1-11	73, 74
1 Thess 5:1-11	71
1 Thess 5:4-9	55
1 Thess 5:6	68
1Thess 5:9	56
1 Thess 5:2,3	14
1 Thess 5:4-10	27
2 Thess 1:5-10	61
2 Thess 1:6-10	28, 71
2 Thess 1:7-9	74
2 Thess 2:1,2	75
2 Thess. 2:1-11	55

Rev 3:10,11	29
Rev 4:1-3	29
Rev 4:1-5,14	62
Rev. 4-18	55
Rev 5:8-10	29
Rev 5:9	56
Rev 6-18	60
Rev 6:1	16
Rev. 6:13-17	73
Rev 6:16,17	16
Rev 7	19
Rev 7:9,14	19
Rev 7:9-17	56
Rev 8:2	66
Rev 11	19
Rev 11:15	66
Rev 11:18	9
Rev 12:2	64
Rev 12:3	64
Rev 12:6	64
Rev 12:12	9
Rev 13:5	64
Rev 13:9	56, 77
Rev 14	19
Rev 14:10	19
Rev. 14:10,11	16
Rev 14:14-20	53
Rev 15:4	16
Rev 16:15,16	53
Rev 16:18-21	17
Rev 19:7-9	30
Rev 19:7-10	62
Rev 19:11-21	54, 72
Rev 22:7	35
Rev 22:12	35
Rev 22:20	35

ABOUT THE AUTHOR

Dr. J. A. Moorman and his wife, Dot. 2017

Jack A. Moorman studied for a while at the Indianapolis campus of Purdue University, attended briefly Indiana Bible College, and graduated from Tennessee Temple Bible School. He has been with Baptist International Missions Inc. (BIMI) since 1967 and has been involved in church planting, Bible Institute teaching and extensive distribution of Scriptures and gospel tracts in Johannesburg, South Africa from 1968 – 1988, and in England and London since 1988. He married his wife, Dot, on November 22 1963.

J.A. Moorman has written the following scholarly books defending the King James Bible and the Hebrew, Aramaic and Greek words that underlie it:

1. When the KJV Departs from the "Majority Text."
2. Early Manuscripts, Church Fathers, and the Authorized Version.
3. Forever Settled

4. Missing in Modern Bibles—The Old Heresy Revived.
5. Samuel P. Tregelles—The Man Who Made the Critical Text Acceptable to Bible Believers.
6. 8,000 Differences Between the Textus Receptus and the Critical Text.
7. Bible Chronology: The Two Great Divides.
8. The Biblical and Observational Case for Geocentricity.

These well-documented works and are replete with evidence which he has gleaned from his own resources as well as references found in the British Museum, British Library and other libraries in South Africa and the United Kingdom.

He has been the pastor of Bethel Baptist Church in London, England since 1993. A great deal of his time, and on a nearly daily basis, is spent in distributing Gospel Literature on the crowded streets of London and beyond. May God bless his unfailing service to the Lord Jesus Christ.

www.ingramcontent.com/pod-product-compliance
Lightning Source LLC
Chambersburg PA
CBHW062010040426
42447CB00010B/1991